MW00614504

BALANCE MATTERS

365 Life Balance Tips!

Marie

Keep the

Balance Always!

Praise for *Balance Matters*

I was fortunate to read Brent's book first thing on a quiet Sunday morning. His ideas elevated my spirits, made me laugh and pumped me up to have one of the greatest weeks of my life. How rare for any book to offer such immediate life-changing and positive benefits.

Dave Lieber, popular *Fort Worth Star-Telegram* Columnist

Everyone deserves a touch of "Circus" in their life—a moment to invite fresh balance to busy lives. Brent O'Bannon has managed to galvanize a series of insights to better achieve that life balance. Readers will be smiling silently as they walk the walk of this impressive series of reflections.

Bob Danzig, former CEO/ Hearst Newspapers/ Speaker/ Author

The sound counsel you provide, is so relevant and timely. Your perspective on life, the many stories and examples you use, and your sense of humor make what you say easy to remember.

Janet Harris, senior editor, Brown Books

Life is naturally unbalanced as we juggle our commitments. Emotional burnout, relationship burnout and success burnout are all so common. Brent's extraordinary book tips the scale back in your favor. It's a practical guide that solves burnout forever.

Mark Berry, Author of *Splatter Dating*, Founder of Love Kung Fu

Brent O'Bannon has boiled down the psychological essentials to a healthy life. Balance Matters serves a batch of mental snacks and practical vitamins that are easy to swallow. Take a daily dose or nibble if you want a balanced life. Any book that quotes Jimmy Buffet can't be half bad!

Ken Myers, Bishop, Christ Church Cathedral

If you are stressed and don't have time to read, you need to read Balance Matters *twice. It's full of juicy tidbits.*
Darren LaCroix, 2001 World champion of Public Speaking

Balance Matters *provides everyone with an excellent roadmap to improving the equilibrium between work, home, play, and relationships. Get this book and get back on the highway to happiness.*
Anne Barab, The Resilience Expert

Balance Matters *is a vibrant new look at the importance of finding that happy place in our lives where we can effectively, even playfully, keep all of life's balls in the air.*
Latham Shinder, Author of The Graffiti Sculptor

As you hold this book in your hands, know that you have discovered the key to unlocking your amazing power and potential. Nature is all about balance. Life is all about balance. If you are going to live your life to fulfill all that you aspire to, this book is going to give you the wisdom and practical steps to getting there. Get it, adopt its message and adapt its principles.
Michael Murphy, author of Powerful Attitudes and Powerfirmations

Having known the author for over 20 years, I have witnessed how he successfully achieves balance in his own life. Brent O'Bannon will give you dynamic tools to improve your life in this fast paced world. Buy Balance Matters as the next book in your library.
Michael Goforth, National Seminars Faculty, President of Big Dream, Inc

Brent's passion, upstanding character, and down-to-earth explanations encourages anyone to feel connected immediately. If Balance Matters *can help me through the emotional lows and highs of a 140 game broadcast schedule in the Texas League of Professional Baseball then I know his 365 life balance tips will also help you.*
Scott Garner, Award-Winning Broadcaster/The voice of the Frisco Roughriders

BALANCE MATTERS

365 Life Balance Tips!

Brent O'Bannon, MBS

Publishing

Balance Matters
365 Life Balance Tips!

© Copyright 2007 by Brent O'Bannon, MBS

First edition, 2007 Business/Self help/Psychology

Published by:

R & B Publishing
115 S. Travis, Suite 303
Sherman, TX 75090, U.S.A.
(903)-813-0723

Book consultant, Latham Shinder	lathamshinder@aol.com
Copy editor, Anita Robeson	asonic@aol.com
Book designer, Janet Long	jlong@eaze.net
Photographer, Lee Clayton	2thkeeper@gmail.com
Grammar editor, Kelli Foster	foster.kelli@gmail.com

ISBN 979-0-9798049-9-1

Published in the United States of America

Contents

About the Author

Brent O'Bannon is a licensed professional counselor and cofounder of Brief Therapy, a successful counseling practice in Sherman, Texas. In more than 20 years as a professional counselor, he has helped hundreds of adolescents, couples, and families reestablish a happy, healthy balance in their lives

O'Bannon holds a master's degree in counseling psychology from Southeastern Oklahoma State University, is a member of the National Speakers Association, and is a Distinguished Toastmaster, the highest recognition a member of Toastmasters may receive. He is a popular international speaker and has spoken to groups at such well-known companies as Cardinal Health, Cigna, J C Penney, Nortel, Tenet Health Systems, and Verizon. He is available as a life coach and speaking coach.

Like many of you he strives to keep the balance in his marriage, stresses to care for his aging mother, and struggles raising two adult children. Often called the "Balance Master" by his fans, he coaches, counsels, speaks, and writes to fulfill his mission of bringing balance to the world.

Acknowledgments

Gratitude unlocks the fullness of life.
It turns what we have into enough, and more.
It turns denial into acceptance, chaos to order,
confusion to clarity. It can turn a meal into
a feast, a house into a home, a stranger into
a friend. Gratitude makes sense of our past,
brings peace for today, and creates a vision
for tomorrow.

Melody Beattie

I would like to share some personal thanks to my life balance team!

Thank You God for forgiving me where I have failed. Thank You for comforting me where I hurt when no one else knows my pain. Thank You for waking my spirit and drawing me back to you when my heart had fallen asleep! Thank You God for an awesome church home and incredible priest. Thank you God for the opportunity to carry on your tradition of writing stories that transform a life!

Thank you Rhonda for not giving up on our marriage when you had good reasons to leave. Thank you for your strength of compassion, loyalty, and willingness to grow! You gave me time, space, and patience when I was stressed to be able to write this book. Your wisdom and insights were enormous.

Thank you Tara and Trent for teaching me more about love, life, and character. I have not always been the best father or raised you the way I should. Thank you for raising me! I hope this book inspires you to keep the balance and to be better than I ever dreamed. You both are destined for greatness!

Thank you to my parents, in laws, and extended family. Mom and Dad you have given me the gift of balance. Thank you for giving me roots to grow and wings to fly. Thank you Joe and Phyllis for giving me space to grow and your willingness to understand me. Thank you Werner family for sharing your heart and life with Tara and Trent. Thank you to all my family for such a diverse, humorous, and accepting heart.

Thank you to my best friend Michael and all of my balance buddies. Michael, you truly understand me, accept me, and encourage me! You were my biggest cheerleader to finally finish my first book. Mike R., Tommy, and Randy thank you for all the laughs on the golf course to keep my sanity while writing a book. Thank you Lee and Barbie for giving your time, knowledge, and inspiration on my many projects.

Thank you to the world's best couple friends. What would Rhonda and I do without you all? Tracy and Sheila, Dwayne and Julie, Mike and Lynn, George and Andrea, Tommy and Sharon, you make us laugh, you make us open up, you hold us accountable.

Thank you to all of my counseling clients, eZine readers, and speaking audience. Thank you for sharing your stories, your heart, your insights. Thank you for your input, your praises, your evaluations, and your belief in what I do.

Thank you to NSA, Toastmasters and Discovery. Thank you NSA members for your soul and substance. Thank you Toastmasters for the journey of friendship, growth, leadership, and communication. Thank you Discovery and all my Discovery family for the heart warming experiences in my life! Thank you Carter for being my Discovery buddy!

Finally, thank you to my professional book team. Latham, my book consultant, you helped me get unstuck on finishing my book. You bought me a book model, spent time sending emails, talking on the phone, and consulting me through the process of birthing *Balance Matters*. Thank you Anita and Kelli for your editing work. Thank you Lee and Barbi for your photography. Thank you Janet for your hard work, diligence, and creativity. I admire how you kept the balance while finishing up the book layout and cover design.

Disclaimer

Book writing is not a quick-get-rich scheme. It's an investment of time and effort. There is no guaranty of success. Writing a book is purely a human endeavor and humans make mistakes. If you find a typographical or content error please email Brent O'Bannon at brent@brentspeaks.com.

The author, the writing team, and publisher have made every effort to ensure accuracy and completeness of the information contained in this book. We assume no responsibility for errors, inaccuracies, omissions, or any inconsistency herein. Any slights of people, places or organizations are unintentional.

The purpose of this book is to educate and entertain. The book is a guide and is not intended to replace direct professional assistance. In fact you are encouraged to meet with a professional if you experience any psychological distress. The author and R&B Publishing shall have neither liability nor responsibility to any person or entity with respect to any loss or damage caused or alleged to be caused directly or indirectly by the information contained in this book.

If you do not wish to be bound by the above disclaimer, you may return this book to the publisher for a full refund.

Authors Introduction

Imagine being at the Worlds Greatest Barnum and Bailey Circus. You're squeezed into the crowd, the lights are dim, the drum rolls, and you're looking high into the air. A performer is walking a death defying balancing act on the tight rope.

That was my memory as a child going to the circus with my grandfather. As an adult my perspective has changed. Life feels like a three ring circus and I'm the silly clown on the tight rope. I feel pressure to succeed, to keep up with technology, to make a difference in the world, to be the sugar daddy for my family all with the attitude of the pope, the smile of Mona Lisa, and of course my marriage has to have the passion of Romeo and Juliet.

It's true that we usually teach what we need to learn. I admit that I'm on a journey to create better life balance. My educated guess is that you are trying to lead a more balanced life. Your life may feel like a circus and you feel the pressure to walk your tight rope with success.

My discovery in my own life is that balance is not always spectacular but it is successful! Life balance is always personal, always professional, and forever playful. Simply, Balance Matters!

In the book you will find four sections. The first is called, "Deep Fried Burnout" This flaming section will cook up insights of having a life without balance. You will better understand why people say, "Stick me with a fork; I'm done!" You will discover why you need balance when you are singeing around the edges. Finally, you will taste burnout from a rare, medium, or well done perspective.

The second section is, "Personal Balance." We will discover the balance ultimatum and why balance matters. We will better balance our physical self when we talk how balance is more than a beer in each hand. While looking through the psychological lens we will discover how balance is a mind game. Off we will go and socialize to learn the balance two-step. Just as we fly with a purpose driven life we will learn to soar spiritually with a balance driven life.

The third section is, "Professional Balance." This section will help you take this job and love it. Then we will show how professionals lead with Es. The final inning of professional balance rallies with Brent's top 10 winning ways at work.

The fourth and last section of the book is "Playful Balance." Life balance is not complete without more laughter, play, and joy. If you're too serious I will show you how to lighten up, climb off the treadmill of seriousness, and jump on the trampoline of playfulness.

You will notice that at the end of each chapter is a quick recap of important points which I call, "ON BALANCE." You also have been given a place to tune in to the most important radio station in your life at the end of each chapter. It is WIFM (What's in it for me?) This is an excellent way to get involved and write your response to each chapter. Benjamin Franklin brilliantly said, "Tell me and I forget. Teach me and I remember. Involve me and I learn."

SECTION I:

DEEP FRIED BURNOUT

Chapter 1: Stick Me with a Fork; I'm Done!

Early Saturday is the time to relax on my back deck. One morning as I was sitting down to enjoy a strong cup of coffee, my cell phone rang. A client who was working 80 hours a week, struggling as a single parent with two children, taking care of his aging mother, coaching his kids' soccer team, and serving as a deacon in his church was contemplating suicide. He was burned out to the max. He was fried. Trying to soften his pain with humor, he declared, "Stick me with a fork; I'm done!"

Life *can* sometimes be one flaming-hot grill. If we are left on the grill too long we can get overcooked, losing our tenderness and our juice for life.

Without intending to, my client had demonstrated in his life the many faces of burnout. Are you burned out?

JOB BURNOUT

According to various reports:

- Eighty-one percent of people are unhappy with their work/life balance.
- Forty percent of Americans say work is stressful.
- Twenty-five percent say work is their No. 1 stress.
- One in three Americans is chronically overworked.
- The Japanese government reports 10,000 cases a year of *karoshi* — death by overwork.
- Twenty-three percent of British men feel stressed and anxiety-ridden at the office.
- Sixty percent of Scots want a job that better provides work/life balance.

Are YOU experiencing job burnout?

MARRIAGE/RELATIONSHIP BURNOUT

More than 50 percent of marriages end in divorce. Many couples are simply burned out. They feel bored, betrayed, hurt, incompatible, stuck, unhappy, or unloved. They finally have had enough and say, "I'm done!"

Are YOU experiencing marriage/relationship burnout?

PARENT BURNOUT

Caring for children, teens, adult children, and grandchildren in today's world is tremendously stressful. Parents and grandparents, feeling pressure to be "super parents," work day and night to keep their children on a healthy path. Strained finances plus kids' negative behavior and substance abuse can cause extra tension and strife.

Are YOU experiencing parent burnout?

CAREGIVER BURNOUT

Many people must become caregivers for their aging parents, sick family members, or friends. With both kids and parents to take care of, they're the "sandwich generation." Despite good intentions, these caregivers are plagued by financial and emotional stress, demands on their time, guilt, and compassion fatigue.

Are YOU experiencing caregiver burnout?

VOLUNTEER BURNOUT

Volunteerism is at an all-time high. Many people enjoy giving time and energy to serve as coaches or as mentors, or to do the mundane tasks that are the backbone of many organizations. But the enjoyment of volunteering can turn into resentment when too much is asked of too few. People feel guilty when they want to take a few months off, reduce their role, or quit altogether.

Are YOU experiencing volunteer burnout?

SPIRITUAL BURNOUT

People who seek meaning and purpose in their lives can become involved in spiritual activities to the point of burnout. They can become disillusioned with God and confused in their understanding of spirituality.

Are YOU experiencing spiritual burnout?

EMOTIONAL BURNOUT

Sadly, burnout can lead to deep depression. The emotions become a roller coaster of extremes, leading a person to feel "fried," to give up, and even to attempt suicide.

Are YOU experiencing emotional burnout?

Many people ask what led me to become a professional counselor. My journey began at age 18, when I felt a call to become a minister and began serving my church and community. When our care pastor became sick, the church gave me the opportunity to speak in nursing homes and give devotionals to patients at the famous Menninger Hospital in Topeka, Kansas. During college, I served in campus ministry and as a summer missionary.

Eventually, I became the senior youth pastor of Glad Tidings Church in Sherman, Texas. These were four marvelous years of serving, counseling, teaching, organizing, and playing with youth and their parents.

But I became discontented. I was ready for the challenge of serving as senior pastor of a church. Maybe because of my prying, a door was opened and I became the senior pastor of the Open Door Church in Topeka Kansas. By then, I had a wife and two toddlers, and they moved with me to Topeka.

After serving as pastor for a year, the church board asked me to resign. Some felt I was too progressive and that my beliefs were too different from theirs. I was hurt, confused, and devastated.

My wife and I quickly moved back to Texas and returned to the church where I had been the youth pastor.

Then the unspeakable happened. I was not aware of my work burnout, did not seek help, and had a lapse of moral character. I was embarrassed. I was ashamed. I felt like a looser in life. In my heart, I felt the words that a client would later speak to me: "Stick me with a fork; I'm done!"

If the stresses in your life seem overwhelming, it's time to look in the mirror and ask, "Mirror, mirror, on the wall; who's the most burned out of all?" If you think it might be you, take the inventory below with an open, honest heart.

BRENT'S BURNOUT INVENTORY
Check any symptoms you've had in the last six months.

DEPLETED
❏ I feel physically exhausted.
❏ I feel restless.
❏ I feel emotionally exhausted.
❏ I feel prone to illness.
❏ I have poor concentration.
❏ I have sleep problems.
❏ I feel overwhelmed with life's problems.

Total _____

DISCONNECTED
❏ I feel that people are a hassle.
❏ I have lost my connection with people.
❏ I treat people as objects.
❏ I have lost my empathy for people.
❏ I feel more cynical about people.
❏ I feel there's little hope for people.
❏ People blame me for their problems.

Total _____

DEFLATED
❏ My job is a dead-end career.
❏ I lack support at my job.
❏ I feel powerless at my job.
❏ I feel unappreciated at my job.
❏ I lack passion for my job.
❏ I have lost desire to learn in my work.
❏ I'm at the end of my rope in my job.

Total _____

Total of all three categories _____

To score, count the number of symptoms you've checked.
1-7   Low burnout (The flame is flickering.)
8-14   Moderate burnout (The flame is out.)
15-21   High burnout (Ashes to ashes, dust to dust.)

Looking deeper into the mirror (your score):

- If you had more symptoms under the depleted category you are most likely experiencing physical, mental, and emotional exhaustion. You are most likely under tremendous pressure and you are experiencing the wear and tear of stress. The antidote is to practice positive coping strategies with stress.

- If you had more symptoms under the disconnected category you are most likely struggling caring about people. You are most likely experiencing a form of compassion fatigue. Your burnout has more to do with a lack of heart felt connection with people. The antidote is to renew and develop relationships in your life.

- If you had more symptoms under the deflated category you are most likely bored or overwhelmed with work. You are most likely working in an unbalanced work culture or lacking purpose in your work and life. The antidote is to help grow a balanced work culture and discover your purpose in life.

Tip 1
You can't fix what you don't face.

— Admit to yourself and one other person where you're unbalanced or burned out.

ON BALANCE:

- Burnout usually happens to the driven not the lazy.
- There are many types of burnout.
- It is dangerous to be in denial about burnout.
- There are three parts to burnout.

WHAT'S IN IT FOR ME?

_____

_____

_____

_____

_____

Chapter 2: Singeing Around the Edges

Burnout is a drain on all aspects of life: personal, family, and work. Burnout is not just an American problem but an international epidemic. Sixty percent of work absences in the U.S. and abroad are due to psychological problems — that equals $57 billion a year.

If you're burning out or maybe just singeing around the edges we need to talk about burnout for three reasons.

HEAL THYSELF

A speaker shared this story of an elderly lady who was burned out. She had worked 30-plus years and was ready for some fun. Her first adventure was a trip to Colorado, where she went white-water rafting. But when she came to her first rapids, she capsized. A man on the riverbank grabbed at her, but instead ripped her shirt off. The woman continued downriver in a panic. The man ran alongside and grabbed her by the hair, but her hair pulled out. At last he was able to grab her by the arm, but her arm fell off. In frustration he said, "If I'm going to help you, lady, you're going to have to pull yourself together!"

I love this cheesy story because it reminds us that we're all human and need to take responsibility for pulling ourselves together.

It's been said, "Physician, heal thyself." It can also be said, "Professional, heal thyself." We need to practice what we preach.

To quote the great psychologist Carl Rogers: "I have always been better at caring for others than caring for myself, but in these later years I'm making progress."

My wife and I were paying for our daughter and son to go to the dentist and orthodontist. One day we realized we had not been to the dentist ourselves in 10 years. Yikes! The good news is that I had become friends with a dentist through Toastmasters, and we started going to him for regular checkups.

Tip 2
You are the
key to your
success.

— *Take care of one area in your life you have neglected.*

DO NO HARM

What is the No. 1 responsibility of a doctor? At the least, to do no harm. Parents, teachers, counselors, medical personnel, ministers, law enforcement — we ALL have an ethical responsibility to beat burnout and balance our lives. When we allow burnout to remain in our lives, we harm the people we live and work with.

Recently a counselor hit the brick wall of burnout. He had served and counseled his clients for twenty years. He was struggling with his marriage. When they separated, he did not show up the next day to see his clients. In fact he moved to a different town without calling his clients and never entered the counseling profession again. I'm sure his hurting clients felt abandoned and the counselor's burnout added harm to his clients.

— Give a written or verbal thank you to a caring professional in your life.

BOOST MORALE

Morale in the workplace, in government organizations, and in many families is incredibly low. Morale affects our level of confidence in, enthusiasm for, and loyalty to a group or organization. What is your workplace morale?

Did you hear the story of the man who finally retired? He was asked by the company CEO, "What he would he like to do in his retirement?" The man stated he would like to spend more time with his wife, go golfing, and play with his grandchildren. The CEO said, "You don't have any grandchildren." The man replied, "You asked me what I wanted to do."

That night the entire family was at the dinner table. The retired husband with his wife and the adult children with their spouses were gathered together. Everyone bowed their head and the newly retired man prayed, "Lord, thank you for this food. Thank you for my new retirement. Lord I especially thank you for my first grandchild who will get one million dollars in their savings account when they are born. Again thank you for all these blessings." When the retired man looked up, except for his wife the table was empty. Now that is one way to increase motivation and boost morale!

— Treat a co-worker to lunch.

Tip 3
Treat others the way you want to be treated.

Tip 4
Work is like family.

ON BALANCE:
- Anyone can fall apart.
- Everyone is responsible to pull themselves together.
- Burnout is toxic and harms others.
- Burnout zaps workplace morale.

WHAT'S IN IT FOR ME?

_____

_____

_____

_____

_____

Chapter 3: Rare, Medium, or Well Done?

The term burnout was coined in the early 1970s by Herbert Freudenberger, a drug-abuse counselor in New York City. Drug abusers were often called "burnouts" because they fried their brains on drugs and lost life balance. Later, Freudenberger wrote an article on staff burnout that focused on practitioners who, because they too felt "fried," lost their motivation for working with drug abusers.

The 1980s spawned research on burnout in the "high-touch" fields (teaching, counseling, social work, medicine, etc.). The mother of burnout research is Christina Maslach. She applied burnout to the general workforce and defined it as "a syndrome of emotional exhaustion, depersonalization, and reduced personal accomplishment that can occur among individuals who work with people in some capacity."

In my 15 years of professional counseling (that is, in my practice as a psychotherapist), I have heard the theme of burnout from many of my clients: the professional whose life is singeing around the edges, the parent who feels fried, and the unhappy spouse who cries,

"I'm done! I'm done! I'm so done!!!"

Burnout causes people to be depleted, disconnected, and deflated. My question for you is, "Is your burnout rare, medium, or well done?"

DEPLETED

My son and I enjoy playing father/son doubles in tennis tournaments. We were excited about playing in a big tournament in Austin, Texas, as the No. 1 ranked duo. The temperature was 100-plus degrees and the humidity was high. I played my first match in singles and barely prevailed in a three-set, three-hour match. I then played the No. 1 seed and lost a hard-fought two sets.

We had to drive across town to play our father/son match. I really needed some Gatorade, so we stopped at a convenience store. As I started into the store, my legs began to cramp. Feeling embarrassed, I walked back outside, then fell to the ground with strong cramps in my stomach. In a flash my entire body was cramping.

I was one weekend-warrior dad who was dehydrated and burned to a crisp. Finally I allowed my son to call an ambulance. I was given an IV of glucose in the ambulance, then hospitalized for eight hours. The doctors gave me 13 bags of glucose! If I hadn't gotten medical attention when I did, the staff told me, I would have had kidney failure.

I was dehydrated. I was exhausted. I was depleted! Burnout can have that devastating of an effect.

— Give yourself a stress checkup every three months.

SIGNS OF DEPLETION

Check the ones that apply to you.

Tip 5
You get what you inspect, not what you expect.

PHYSICAL
❑ Fatigue and general weakness
❑ Increased restlessness and agitation
❑ Sudden crying spells
❑ Changes in appetite and circadian-rhythm patterns
❑ Increase in number and severity of headaches
❑ Unusual pains in muscles and joints
❑ Sudden muscle cramps and twitches
❑ Changes in sexual interest and sexual energy
❑ Changes in physical ability to engage in sexual behavior
❑ Presence of vomiting, dizziness, chest pains, muscle tremors
❑ Instances of unusual sweating or breathing difficulties
❑ Increase in sudden rapid heart rate and heart rhythm
❑ Increased or decreased blood pressure
❑ Heightened startle response
❑ Sleep disturbances

EMOTIONAL
❑ Numbing of responsiveness to self and to environment
❑ Increase in emotional reactivity
❑ Feeling of general loss of control
❑ Anxiety and apprehension without focus
❑ Increase in generalized irritability and anger
❑ Irrational feelings of helplessness and hopelessness
❑ Exaggerated feelings of guilt, anxiety, fear, depression, etc.
❑ Increase in interpersonal conflict and miscommunication
❑ Sudden emotional outbursts
❑ Guilt feelings about one's actions
❑ Mood swings

❑ Increase in feelings of vulnerability, sadness, craziness
❑ Loss of interest in usual pleasurable activities

COGNITIVE
❑ Concentration problems
❑ Short- and long-term memory problems
❑ Decreased attention span
❑ Decreased ability to learn new material
❑ Lowering of thinking and abstraction skills
❑ Increase in lack of confidence in oneself
❑ Rumination and intrusive thoughts
❑ Obsessive thoughts
❑ Feelings of unreality
❑ Confusion
❑ Difficulty in decision making
❑ Making poor judgments
❑ Hyper vigilance
❑ Increase in suspicion and distrust of things and people
❑ Changes in perception of time, place, and person
❑ Difficulty identifying objects and people
❑ Increased or decreased awareness of surroundings
❑ Increase in superstitious beliefs
❑ Increase in externalizing blame for problems

BEHAVIORAL
❑ Increased risk of causing accidents
❑ Increased likelihood of acting violently
❑ Withdrawal from social interaction
❑ Work productivity problems
❑ Increase in absenteeism
❑ Premature resignation and early retirement
❑ Increase in experiencing common illnesses
❑ Increased use of medical services
❑ Regressive actions and reactions
❑ Increased difficulty communicating facts, feelings, and desires
❑ Increased use of alcohol and drugs (both prescribed and illicit)
❑ Increase in antisocial acts

❏ Inability to rest or to profit from periods of rest
❏ Change in social behavior patterns
❏ Increase in arguments and conflicts with others
❏ Change in patterns of personal hygiene

DISCONNECTED

When people get burned out, they lose connection with self, family, friends, and customers. Our true self is hidden behind a shell. We wear a mask showing only what we want others to see. I felt this disconnection when I was writhing in pain with dehydration and cramps after playing tennis. People walked in and out of the store without even making eye contact. No one asked if I needed help. They probably thought I was a drug addict tweaking on crack. I was a fellow human being needing a helping hand.

A friend sent me an e-mail picture of a Marine sniper in Iraq. The CNN reporter who had interviewed the sniper had asked, "What do you feel when you shoot people?" "Recoil," the Marine replied. The soldier had learned to disconnect with his own feelings of empathy and sympathy. He had a job to do, so he did it.

It is easy to simply go through the motions in our work and in our lives. We can easily grow disconnected and treat customers, patients, clients, and prospects as objects and not real people.

— *Write a letter to yourself expressing how you feel about the people you are disconnected from.*

Tip 6
No pain, no gain.

DEFLATED

My son and I were deflated when we had to forfeit the father/son match at the Austin tournament. We had been winning throughout the year, and now we could only watch on the sideline, wishing we were on the court.

Burnout leads to a loss of personal and professional effectiveness. You feel like you have lost your winning edge. You feel like you are not on top of your game. You feel demoralized. Like a tire that has lost its air, balance, and effectiveness, you feel deflated.

Tip 7
Misery loves company.

— Share with someone who has experienced deflation as you have.

BRENT'S TOP 10 SIGNS OF BURNOUT, DAVID LETTERMAN STYLE

You know you're burned out when . . .

10. You get to work and it's your day off.
9. Your phone is always on "do not disturb."
8. You start planning your sick leave for a 3-day weekend.
7. You spend all day at work looking for another job.
6. You treat department food fests like national holidays.
5. Your son is walking around in a dress and you don't care.
4. You are a frequent caller to the Dr. Phil show.
3. Oncoming traffic looks attractive.
2. You have Jack Daniels instead of coffee.

Drum roll please . . .

You know you're burned out when . . .

1. Your co-worker calls in sick and you say, "Thank God!"

Tip 8
"If we didn't laugh we would all go insane."
— Jimmy Buffet

— LOL (Laugh o' little and e-mail your funny line to Brent at brent@brentspeaks.com)

ON BALANCE:

- Burnout is a syndrome.
- Burnout has physical, emotional, cognitive, and behavioral signs.
- Burnout creates disconnection with self and others.
- Burnout leads to a loss of personal and professional effectiveness.

WHAT'S IN IT FOR ME?

_____

_____

_____

_____

_____

SECTION II:

PERSONAL BALANCE

Chapter 4: The Balance Ultimatum

Balance is the antidote to burnout Life has an ultimatum. Do we want to live a life of burnout or balance? We have broken burnout into its three elements: depleted, disconnected, and deflated. Now, let's get a vision of what constitutes balance: energy, engagement, and effectiveness.

> **BURNOUT vs. BALANCE**
> **DEPLETED vs. ENERGIZED**
> **DISCONNECTED vs. ENGAGEMENT**
> **DEFLATED vs. EFFECTIVE**

BALANCE IS ENERGY

Wouldn't you love to have the physical, mental, emotional, and spiritual energy to accomplish all that you want in life? Burnout zaps your life energy, but balance boosts your ability to tackle any task, great or small. How do you increase your energy? Sleep.

I ventured to the mall recently to get a long-overdue haircut.

While getting my shampoo and spring highlights, I fell fast asleep. "You must have really needed that," my hairdresser said. I stretched, yawned, opened my eyes, and said, "I guess I did."

I know you should let sleeping dogs lie, but do you realize that sleep is vital to life balance?

One-half of American adults experience some insomnia.

Eleven percent of Americans use prescription or over-the-counter medication to help them sleep.

Seventy percent of shift workers experience sleep disturbances.

Ninety percent of people with depression and anxiety have a hard time sleeping.

Sleep deprivation can cause car accidents. It can impair judgment on the job and emotional functioning in social and family relationships.

Tips 9-15 Let sleeping dogs lie. — *Open your eyes to these seven suggestions for getting a good night's sleep.*

• **Tip 9 Wake up at the same time every morning,** regardless of how much you slept. Follow the same relaxing, going-to-bed routine. For example, wash your face, brush your teeth, read a magazine, meditate, listen to music, or pray.

• **Tip 10 If you are unable to fall asleep after 15-20 minutes,** get up and go to another room and engage in an activity (reading, writing, folding clothes, etc.) until you get sleepy. The worst thing you can do is to "toss and turn" in bed.

• **Tip 11 De-clutter, decorate, and design your bedroom for sleep and sex.** Don't allow your bedroom to become an office, a workout room, or a storage closet. Decorate and design your bedroom to become a relaxing oasis that is associated with peace, pleasure, and privacy.

- **Tip 12 Exercise daily and increase your physical activity.** This decreases sedentary behavior and allows for deeper sleep.

- **Tip 13 Do not nap.** Naps reduce the quality and quantity of sleep. Take breaks to refresh yourself.

- **Tip 14 Eat a light, nutritional snack before going to bed.** Research shows that foods with L-tryptophan (like turkey or milk) help induce sleep. Eliminating hunger will improve sleep.

- **Tip 15 Avoid alcohol, caffeine, tobacco, and the overuse of sleeping pills.** Every one of these will decrease sleep quality. The continued use of sleep medication has been found to decrease the quality of sleep. Consult your doctor.

A friend recently called me in a panic and shared how overwhelmed he was. He had been burning the candle at both ends and was exhausted. It's been said, "If you snooze you loose," but in the game of life balance, "You must rest for your best." Balance is energy!

BALANCE IS ENGAGEMENT

Burnout leads to disconnection with yourself and others. You don't have enough energy to take the time to connect heart to heart. My work as a professional counselor is all about connecting with my clients. But having client after client day after day, week after week, month after month can cause compassion fatigue. Anyone who is in a "high-touch" field or has a lot of contact with people needs to keep his or her heart connection fresh. I call this engagement.

One day this incredible connection and engagement became clear. A single mother and her 6-year-old son struggling with behavior problems came to my counseling office. The hyperactive boy bebopped in, bouncing off the walls like a Tasmanian devil. After plopping down in the middle of the floor, he pulled from his backpack two pieces of paper from the school office and gave them to his mother. "I don't want to get in trouble, Mama," he said, beginning to cry. "Please, Mama, I don't want to get in trouble."

The exhausted mom got up from her chair, walked over to her son, and placed her hands gently around his face. She massaged his back while looking into his eyes and said, "Everyone has good days and bad days. Who is the sunshine of my life?" The little boy's expression instantly changed and he joyfully said, "I am, Mama."

The connection and affection between that mother and son was amazing. My heart was exhilarated to see this kind of heart-to-heart engagement. That mother gave unconditionally to her son and impacted his self-esteem and life.

Tips 16-22
"Those who bring sunshine to the lives of others cannot keep it from themselves."
— James Barrie

— Use this CONNECT acronym to engage heart to heart with people

• **Tip 16 C**are

• **Tip 17 O**pen body language

• **Tip 18 N**otice the needs and passion

• **Tip 19 N**od

• **Tip 20 E**ye contact

• **Tip 21 C**hildlike playfulness

• **Tip 22 T**ouch

BALANCE IS EFFECTIVE

My wife and I went skiing in Monarch, Colorado, after a 19-year hiatus. I was hesitant at first because, at age 41, I thought I would get "dangerous" on the slopes and break a few bones. But the couple we traveled with was enthusiastic about skiing, so away we went.

Balance is a lot like coming down those slippery slopes. The more I skied the more curious I got about how people kept their balance while skiing. I thought of three kinds of skiers. Which one do you identify with? Which one is most effective?

First is the snow-plow skier. My wife started out like this. As she came down the slope her eyes looked straight down at her skis and she missed the beautiful view of the mountains. She did not pick up any speed because she didn't want to fall. She was overly cautious. She snow-plowed all the way down the mountain. She played it safe.

The second kind is the speedster. I was amazed at how little children and teenagers would zoom down the slopes without poles or fear. They were not afraid of falling. In fact, they seemed to welcome the opportunity to fall.

Number three is the smooth skier. These skiers came down the slopes with speed, simplicity, and serenity. They nicely balanced both the journey and the challenge.

— *Slow down, follow the speed limit, pay attention, and drive effectively.*

**Tip 23
Drive your vehicle like you want to live your life.**

What kind of balance do you have in your life? How do you slide down life's slippery slopes?

Are you like the snow-plow skier who goes into life with no eye contact? Are you cautious, mistrustful, and afraid of making a fool of yourself? You're not enjoying your life, your work, your co-workers, or your customers. You're afraid of failure.

Do you dive in head-first like the speedster, racing through life and work oblivious to the people around you? Are you so focused on getting in and out that you don't make life and work meaningful?

Or have you learned how to be the smooth skier who opens his eyes and lives life with purpose? Do you know when to speed up and when to slow down? Can you glide along knowing you will fall, yet not give up?

Believe me, I'm not the expert skier. I began very cautiously, and by watching my friend I learned as the day went on how to ski more freely. I took a few more risks to ski faster, go through some trees, and jump a few hills. Of course I fell down, and had fun doing so. At the same time I was finding my personal balance on the slippery slopes. Now I want to go skiing every year!

Find your personal balance on the slippery slopes of work, and you will live and work with speed, simplicity, and serenity. Balance is effective!

ON BALANCE:

- Balance helps you rest for your best.
- Balance is connection.
- Connection is like sunshine.
- Balance is like a smooth skier.

WHAT'S IN IT FOR ME?

_____

_____

_____

_____

_____

Chapter 5: Balance is More than a Beer in Each Hand

Have you ever wondered how to climb the ladder of personal success without getting all rung out?

A man's got to do what his mind tells him to. So I climbed 45 scary feet to the top rung and tied off the ladder so it wouldn't fall in the swirling wind. I climbed back down and started my chainsaw. Up, up, and away I climbed again, trembling in my boots, determined to cut the gnarly branches that blocked the sunlight from my swimming pool.

Whether you're trimming trees in your back yard, climbing the corporate ladder, or just trying to live from the treetops like Tarzan and Jane, personal success takes a balance of the physical, mental, social, and spiritual.

PHYSICAL BALANCE

You know that to climb a ladder four-and-a-half stories high in a swirling wind with a running 15-pound chainsaw takes physical coordination, strength, and stamina. Life balance begins with physical coordination, strength, and stamina. Our physical life is made up of our health, weight, appearance, sexuality, energy, and exercise.

Did you realize that not drinking enough water is the No. 1 trigger of daytime fatigue? Most people suffer from chronic dehydration. A mere 2 percent drop in body water can trigger fuzzy memory, irritability, and lack of focus. If you want to restore physical balance, read and practice these top 10 tips about drinking water. Remember, balance is more than a beer in each hand.

Tips 24-33
Water is life.

• **Tip 24 Drinking water helps you loose weight.** Drinking 8-10 glasses of water decreases appetite and increases metabolism and digestion.

• **Tip 25 Drinking water flushes out toxins.** Soft drinks, tea, and alcohol are diuretics that dehydrate the body. Drinking water flushes out the kidneys and liver.

• **Tip 26 Drinking water lubricates joints and muscles.** Drinking water before and after exercise helps prevent muscle cramps and increase lubrication in joints.

• **Tip 27 Drinking water helps maintain healthier skin.** Water moisturizes skin from the inside out. Water is a great way to stave off wrinkles and increase elasticity.

• **Tip 28 Drinking water helps you stay regular.** Water makes bowel movements softer and helps prevent constipation.

- **Tip 29 Drinking water regulates body temperature.** You can burn more calories when drinking extra-cold or extra-hot water.

- **Tip 30 Drinking water increases energy.** Water makes up 85 percent of the brain, 80 percent of blood, and 70 percent of lean muscle. Water increases alertness, focus, and strength.

- **Tip 31 Drinking water decreases the risk of heart attack.** Research at Loma Linda University found that people who drank five or more glasses a day of water were less likely to die of a heart attack or heart disease.

- **Tip 32 Drinking water fights sickness.** Drinking more water decreases the chance of getting kidney stones and urinary tract infections, and controls fever.

- **Tip 33 Drinking water needs to be balanced.** Drinking too much water can create a dangerous water intoxication. A person can become addicted — an "aquaholic." Drinking too little water causes chronic cellular dehydration. Drink a balanced amount of water at all times.

Physical balance also includes weight management, exercise, and nutrition.

**Tip 34
Watch your
weight.**

— Here's how to find your Body Mass Index (BMI), which gives you important information about your body.

1. Write down your weight in pounds (example: 190)   _____

2. Multiply that number by 703 (190 x 703 = 133,570)   X_____

3. Multiply your height in inches by itself (70 x 70 = 4,900)   X_____

4. Divide the answer to number 2 by the answer to number 3   ÷_____ (133,570 divided by 4,900 = 27.26)

This is your BMI.

BMI categories:

Under 18.5: **underweight**
18.5-24.9: **normal weight**
25-29.9: **overweight**
30 and above: **obese**

Risk of Associated Disease According to BMI and Waist Size			
BMI		Waist less than or equal to 40 inches (men) or 35 inches (women)	Waist greater than 40 inches (men) or 35 inches (women)
18.5 or less	Underweight	—	N/A
18.5 - 24.9	Normal	—	N/A
25.0 - 29.9	Overweight	Increased	High
30.0 - 34.9	Obese	High	Very high
35.0 - 39.9	Obese	Very High	Very high
40 or greater	Extremely obese	Extremely high	Extremely high

Source: Partnership for Healthy Weight Management

— Work into your life some of these 23 practical ways to exercise.

**Tips 35-57
Exercise
for life.**

- **Tip 35 Take the stairs instead of the elevator.**
- **Tip 36 Park farther away from the office, the grocery store, etc.**
- **Tip 37 Work in the garden.**
- **Tip 38 Cut the grass with a push mower instead of a riding mower.**
- **Tip 39 Go for a short walk before breakfast, after dinner, or both.**
- **Tip 40 Walk to do errands that are a few blocks away.**
- **Tip 41 Pedal a stationary bike or do sit-ups or push-ups while watching TV.**
- **Tip 42 Walk the dog.**
- **Tip 43 Walk down the hall to talk to someone at work instead of calling or e-mailing.**
- **Tip 44 Walk while waiting for a plane at the airport.**
- **Tip 45 Take a walk at lunch and brainstorm ideas with a friend.**
- **Tip 46 When golfing, walk instead of using a cart.**
- **Tip 47 Carry your own groceries.**
- **Tip 48 Do housework at a brisk pace.**
- **Tip 49 Wash your car yourself.**
- **Tip 50 For every hour of computer time, move briskly for 5 minutes.**
- **Tip 51 Play actively with your kids, grandchildren, or pets.**

- **Tip 52 Use the exercise equipment you already own.**
- **Tip 53 Plan family activities such as canoeing, swimming, or skiing.**
- **Tip 54 Break up long drives by hiking nature trails and scenic walks.**
- **Tip 55 Sweep the sidewalk, clean the windows, or clean out the garage or basement.**
- **Tip 56 Rake the leaves.**
- **Tip 57 Take a brisk walk around the office several times a day.**

What excuse do you use for not exercising? Do you need a solution to help you exercise?

Tips 58-65 Make exercise a lifelong habit.

— Weigh these excuses for not exercising, then size up my solutions.

- **Tip 58** It's inconvenient. **Make it as convenient as possible** (e.g., try an exercise date for lunch).
- **Tip 59** I don't have time. **Schedule exercise as an appointment.** Exercise while you do some other task.
- **Tip 60** It's boring. **Make your routine fun, and vary the activities, time, and place.**
- **Tip 61** It's hard to keep it up. **Build in a reward system.** It takes a little time for the intrinsic rewards of exercise to be satisfying.

- **Tip 62** I'm too out of shape. **Start slowly.** Know that you are reaping rewards long before the scale shows it. Meanwhile, focus on the other ways it improves your health.

- **Tip 63** I've tried and failed before. It takes four to six weeks before aerobic capacity is improved. **Set smaller, reachable goals first.** Focusing on the small steps that you can manage will eventually lead to your ultimate goal.

- **Tip 64** I hate jogging. Don't jog. **Any physical movement is better than none at all.** Pick what you are most comfortable with — walking, dancing, roller skating, cycling, swimming, etc.

- **Tip 65** It's painful. **If it hurts, you're doing something wrong.** Check your technique, or find a less strenuous activity. Cycling? Walking? Swimming? Dancing?

Take a closer look at your nutrition. Think about your typical eating patterns and food decisions.

Tip 66
You are what
you eat.

— *Rate your plate by giving yourself points for your answers.*

Rate Your Plate			
Do you...	Usually	Sometimes	Never
Consider nutrition when you make food choices?	2	1	0
Try to eat regular meals (including breakfast) rather than skip or skimp on some?	2	1	0
Choose nutritious snacks?	2	1	0
Try to eat a variety of foods?	2	1	0
Include new-to-you foods in meals and snacks?	2	1	0
Try to balance your energy intake (calories) with your physical activity?	2	1	0
Eat more whole-grain than refined-grain products?	2	1	0
Eat at least 3 servings* of vegetables daily?	2	1	0
Eat at least 2 servings* of fruits daily?	2	1	0
Consume at least 2 servings* of milk, yogurt, or cheese daily?	2	1	0
Go easy on saturated fats, and moderately on polyunsaturated and monounsaturated fats?	2	1	0
Go easy on sweets?	2	1	0
Drink 8 or more cups of fluids daily?	2	1	0
Limit alcoholic beverages (no more than 1 daily For a woman or 2 for a man)?	2	1	0

*Serving sizes vary depending on the food and food group

Score yourself by adding up your points.

❏ **24 or more:** Healthful eating seems to be your fitness habit already. Still, look for ways to stick to a healthful eating plan — and to make a "good thing" even better.

❏ **16 to 23:** You're on track. A few easy changes could help you make your overall eating plan healthier.

❏ **9 to 15:** Sometimes you eat smart, but not often enough to be at your "fitness best."

❏ **0 to 8:** For your good health, you'd be wise to rethink your overall eating style. Take it gradually, step by step. Make moves for healthful eating. Gradually turn your "nevers" into "sometimes" and your "sometimes" into "usually."

Adapted from *The American Dietetic Association's Monthly Nutrition Companion: 31 Days to a Healthier Lifestyle*, **Chronimed Publishing, 1997.**

Physical balance is more than a beer in each hand.

ON BALANCE:

• Balance helps you climb the ladder of success without getting rung out.
• Physical balance begins with drinking plenty of water.
• Physical balance uses exercise to help weight management.
• Physical balance eats healthy.

WHAT'S IN IT FOR ME?

_____

_____

_____

_____

_____

Chapter 6: Balance is a Mind Game

Do you want to climb the ladder of success without getting wrung out? Clear the air for more sunlight in your life? Then remember balance is a mind game. To keep good balance in your mental life, notice the difference between thoughts, feelings, and actions.

Thoughts are the bricks and mortar of struggle and of success.

I honestly had — at the same time — thoughts of "I can't climb this ladder" and thoughts of "I can climb this ladder." It is natural to have a battle going between negative and positive self talk. But you must keep repeating the positive, "I can climb the ladder!"

What is your core thinking? Do you say "I can" or "I can't"? Take the first step up the ladder by believing and saying "I can."

What irrational beliefs do you struggle with? Take a look at 12 core irrational beliefs, adapted from *Feeling Good* by David Burns.

**Tips 67-78
You are what
you think.
— Identify your
core irrational
beliefs.**

- **Tip 67 Filtering** Taking the negative details, magnify them while filtering out the positive aspects of the situation.

- **Tip 68 Black-and-white thinking** You see no middle ground (e.g., you view yourself as either perfect or a failure).

- **Tip 69 Overgeneralization** You base your conclusions on one piece of evidence.

- **Tip 70 Mind-reading** You believe you know what people are feeling and why they act the way they do, especially toward you.

- **Tip 71 Catastrophizing** You expect disaster. You specialize in spinning "worst case/what if " scenarios.

- **Tip 72 Personalization** You interpret irrelevant actions as a reaction to you.

- **Tip 73 Control fallacies** You see yourself as a helpless victim of fate, or you feel responsible for everyone else.

- **Tip 74 Blaming** You hold other people responsible for your pain.

- **Tip 75 "Shoulds"** You have a rigid internal list of rules. Rule-breakers make you angry. When you break the rules, you feel guilty.

- **Tip 76 Emotional reasoning** You believe that what you feel must always be true. If you feel stupid, then it must be so.

- **Tip 77 Being right** You are continually trying to prove you're right. You will do anything to demonstrate your rightness.

- **Tip 78 Deserved-reward fallacy** You expect all self-sacrifice to pay off, feeling bitter when others act unfairly or if rewards don't come.

Feelings are different from thoughts and beliefs. Feelings are like the swirling wind; they come and go. Feelings can be pleasant or unpleasant. You cannot stop the wind or feelings, but you can navigate through them carefully. Anchor your feelings to your positive thoughts, like when I tied my ladder to the trunk of the tree to stabilize my ascent. What feelings do you struggle with? Are you more controlled by your thoughts or feelings?

Recently, I felt both sad and mad.

"Don't fret," a friend told me. "It will get better." "It's OK for me to fret for a little while," I told him. "I don't always have to be positive."

Feelings are normal, and everyone will experience a range of emotions. Paul Ekman discovered there are six basic emotions experienced in all cultures: happiness, surprise, sadness, anger, disgust, and fear. His research also discovered that cultures have display rules. These are social and cultural rules about how a person should regulate emotional and facial expressions.

In your family as you were growing up, what was OK and not OK about experiencing and expressing feelings? Did you have permission to feel happiness but not anger? Did you have permission to feel sad and cry, or was there pressure to always be strong and optimistic?

There is a balance in feeling experiences and expression. There is a time to allow yourself to experience pleasant feelings as well as unpleasant feelings. Both sides create meaning, depth, and balance. There is a time to express anger and sadness, just as there are appropriate times to express happiness and pleasure. Some people are out of balance with their feelings. They focus on one extreme or the other.

The wise King Solomon taught (and the Byrds put to music), "There is a time for everything, a season for every activity under heaven, a time to weep, and a time to laugh, a time to mourn and a time to dance, a time to embrace and a time to refrain, a time to search and a time to give up, a time to be silent and a time to speak, a time to tear and a time to mend, a time to love and a time to hate."

Next time I hope my friend says to me, "It's OK to fret; it will get better."

Part of developing mental balance is knowing your-self. Have you ever deeply explored who you are?

(If you would like counseling or coaching from Brent O'Bannon, MBS, LPC, visit his Web site at www.brentspeaks.com, or e-mail him at brent@brentspeaks.com.)

Tip 79
Know thyself.

— *Answer these life-discovery questions. Discuss them with a counselor, coach, minister, or trusted friend.*

MY "WHO AM I?" LIFE-DISCOVERY JOURNAL

1. What has happened in your life that you are especially proud of?

_____

_____

2. Write about your psychological triumphs. Include the periods of stress and duress that you survived and mastered; small events that may still be of great importance to you; significant events from your childhood or the recent past; self-created challenges you met; periods when you felt powerful; your glories and victories; wonderful friendships you maintained; and so on.

_____

_____

3. How have these successes shaped your life?

_____

_____

4. How have they affected the way you think of yourself and your abilities?

_____

_____

5. How have they affected your goals and the things you strive for?

_____

_____

6. What role has pride (that is, feeling proud, being praised, expressing praise for others) played in your life?

_____

_____

7. When you were young, did your parents show you they were proud of you? How?

_____

_____

8. How have other people responded to your accomplishments?

_____

_____

9. Did your parents show you they loved you? How?

_____

_____

10. Was affection readily expressed in your family? If not, what are the effects and implications for your marriage/relationships?

_____

_____

11. What role does pride in your accomplishments play in your marriage?

_____

_____

12. What role do your own strivings have in your marriage?

_____

_____

13. What do you want your partner to know and understand about these aspects of yourself, your past and present, and your plans for the future?

_____

_____

14. How do you show pride in one another?

_____

_____

MY INJURIES AND HEALINGS

1 What difficult events or periods have you gone through?

_____

_____

2. Write about any significant psychological insults and injuries, your losses, disappointments, trials, and tribulations. Include periods of stress and duress, as well as any quieter periods of despair, hopelessness, and loneliness. Also, include any deep traumas you have undergone as a child or adult. Fox example, harmful relationships, humiliating events, even molestation, abuse, rape, or torture.

_____

_____

3. How have you survived these traumas?

_____

_____

4. What are the lasting effects on you?

_____

_____

5. How did you strengthen and heal yourself?

_____

_____

6. How did you address your grievances?

_____

_____

7. How did you revive and restore yourself?

_____

_____

8. How did you gird and protect yourself against this ever happening again?

_____

_____

9. How do these injuries and the ways you protect and heal yourself affect your marriage today?

_____

_____

10. What do you want your partner to know and understand about these aspects of yourself?

_____

_____

MY EMOTIONAL WORLD

1. How did your family express the following when you were a child:

a. Anger

_____

_____

b. Sadness

_____

_____

c. Fear

_____

_____

d. Affection

_____

_____

e. Disgust

_____

_____

f. Happiness

_____

_____

2. During your childhood, did your family have to cope with a particular emotional problem, such as aggression between parents, a depressed parent, or a parent who had emotional wounds?

_____

_____

3. What implications does this have for your marriage and other close relationships (friendships or relationships with your parents, your siblings, your children)?

_____

_____

4. What is your own philosophy about expressing feelings, particularly sadness, anger, fear, pride, and love?

_____

_____

5. Are any of these difficult for you to express or to see expressed by your spouse?

_____

_____

6. What is the basis of your perspective on this?

_____

_____

7. What differences exist between you and your spouse in the area of expressing emotion?

_____

_____

8. What is behind these differences?

_____

_____

9. What are the implications of these differences for you?

_____

_____

MY MISSION AND LEGACY

1. Imagine you are standing in a cemetery looking at your own tombstone. Now write the epitaph you would like to see there. Begin with "Here lies… "

_____

_____

2. Write your own obituary. (It does not have to be brief.) How do you want people to remember you?

_____

_____

3. Now you are ready to write a mission statement for your life. What is the purpose of your life?

_____

_____

4. What is the meaning in the mission?

_____

_____

5. What are you trying to accomplish through your mission?

_____

_____

6. What is your larger struggle in accomplishing your mission?

_____

_____

7. What legacy would you like to leave when you die?

_____

_____

8. What significant goals have you yet to realize? Minor examples are: learning to play the violin, climbing a mountain, and so on

_____

_____

WHO I WANT TO BECOME

Take a moment now to reflect on what you have written. We are all involved in becoming the person we most want to be. In that struggle we all have demons to fight and overcome.

1. Describe the person you want to become.

_____

_____

2. How can you best help yourself become that person?

_____

_____

3. What struggles have you already faced in trying to become that person?

_____

_____

4. What demons in yourself have you fought? Or still have to fight?

_____

_____

5. What would you most like to change about yourself?

_____

_____

6. What dreams have you denied yourself or failed to develop?

_____

_____

7. What do you want your life to be like in five years?

_____

_____

8. What is the story of the kind of person you would like to be?

_____

_____

Remember, mental balance is about thoughts, feelings, and actions (behavior). Actions not only speak louder than words but accomplish more than words. I could think all day long that I could climb that ladder, but that doesn't make it so.

To climb each rung, you have to force one foot in front of the other. Every journey begins with a single step. Every marathon ends with a step. What steps do you need to take to begin? What projects do you need to finish? Keep moving on that ladder for success.

Many of us struggle with action because of procrastination.

Have you finally had enough?

For years, I had a peaceful ceiling fan in my bedroom. But over the last six months, the ceiling fan progressively got squeakier. Though somewhat irritated, my wife and I tolerated the noise.

But one recent night when I was stressed and in need of some sleep relief, the irritating fan kept me awake. At that moment, I had had enough! I jumped out of bed and fumbled through the dark to the garage to get my trusty WD-40, then stood on the bed and sprayed the fan. To my surprise the squawking fan was instantly fixed.

Why did I procrastinate all those months and not fix the fan?

Procrastination is putting off what needs to be done. Why do people procrastinate?

1. Fear of failure

2. Fear of responsibility

3. Cost of time

4. Cost of money

5. Indecision

6. Lack of knowledge

7. Over-commitment

8. Lack of commitment

9. Just don't want to

Do you need to set an appointment with the doctor or dentist? Do you need to back up the computer? Do you need to start or finish the book you've been wanting to write? When will you write that thank-you note? When will you have that much-needed talk?

Tips 80-83 Pummel procrastination.

• **Tip 80 Ask yourself, "What's the best use of my time right now?"**

• **Tip 81 Tackle the biggest and hardest project with small steps.**

• **Tip 82 Go public and get accountability.**

• **Tip 83 My personal favorite: "If I can do it in 2 minutes, do it now."**

If you've had enough screaming procrastination, then jump out of bed and spray your powerful pointer to pummel procrastination!

Balance is a mind game.

ON BALANCE:

- Thoughts are the brick and mortar of struggles and success.
- Feelings are neither good or bad, just pleasant or unpleasant.
- Mental balance knows the strengths, struggles, and purpose of one's life.
- Mental balance knows how to pummel procrastination.

WHAT'S IN IT FOR ME?

_____

_____

_____

_____

_____

Chapter 7: The Balance Two Step

Did I mention that while I was 45 feet in the air at the top of a ladder, with a chain saw, there was a 40-mph wind swirling about? I'm glad I had my ladder tied to the tree.

I failed to mention how stupid I was that day. I was doing the job without anyone else around. My wife and kids were gone, and I didn't even have a friend working with me. That was not smart!

One huge branch I cut crashed back at me, almost throwing me to the ground. The branch was not quiet severed, and it blocked my way back down the ladder.

I was stuck. Finally, an hour later, a neighbor came outside and I was able to get his attention. Jerry and his son brought over their tree cutters and helped me cut the branch and climb down.

I learned the hard way that personal balance takes support. In Texas we call it the two step.

The three primary kinds of support are:

1. Technical support, sometimes called coaching. You get specific advice or know-how. I want to give special credit to my "technical support guru," Dr. Lee Clayton from Denison, Texas. He has helped me create my monthly eZine, my shopping cart, and my products. I couldn't do it without him.

Tips 84-87 Two are better than one.

• **Tip 84** Take my free "Do I need coaching?" test and get your personal results at www.brentspeaks.com.

2. Emotional support, sometimes called counseling/mentoring. You get objective listening, encouragement, and feedback. Many times you can get emotional support from a best friend, a family member, a minister, or a peer, but there are times when we all need a professional counselor. King Solomon said, "Plans fail for lack of counsel, but with many advisers they succeed."

• **Tip 85** Sign up for my free monthly eZine to support your life balance; check it out at www.brentspeaks.com.

• **Tip 86** Take my free "Do I need counseling?" test and get your personal results at www.brentspeaks.com.

3. Practical support, someone who actually "helps" you to accomplish a task. A friend of mine hired an organizational expert to organize his home and office. My father- in-law helped me build my deck. You get the idea. Practical support can be unpaid or paid, but it's always priceless.

• **Tip 87** Call someone to help you fix something at your house that you have neglected.

Remember, asking for help is a sign of strength. Go ahead, I dare you — ask for help!

If it's the most wonderful time of the year…why do 72% of Americans say "they don't feel joyful during the holidays"? Why do more heart attacks take place in December and January than any other time of the year?

HOLIDAY STRESS

Holiday stress brings intense pressures, relationship conflicts and life changes. Holidays for many become a depressing "Ho hum". For others (dad this is for you) the inner scrooge barks out "Bah hum bug". Of course many of Santa's helpers are exhausted with the "holidaze"! If you feel the pressure of being the Holiday CEO, the conflict of dealing with a blended family, the sadness of loosing a loved one, or the crunch of finances then read and follow my holidaze survival guide.

- **Tip 88** If you experience PME (precious moments expectations) remember that holidays are imperfect. Adjust your unrealistic expectations. Let go of the Norman Rockwell fantasies and let you and others be fully human. They are anyway!

Tips 88-97 Follow a holidaze survival guide.

- **Tip 89** Give yourself permission to face and feel your feelings. Pleasant or unpleasant feelings are both okay and a part of life. Use the AAA method of dealing with feelings. Be AWARE of your feelings, ACCEPT all feelings and ACKNOWLEDGE your feelings to someone you trust.

- **Tip 90** Re-evaluate your traditions. Which holiday traditions do you and your families enjoy and want to continue? Which traditions are done out of ritual and obligation but do not promote holiday happiness? Some traditions are too stressful and time consuming. You have to get rid of the old to make room for the new.

- **Tip 91** Balance your own needs with the needs of others (family, friends, community, etc.) Practice this affirmation to help. Say out loud to yourself daily. "My needs and wants are just as important as yours". The other side of the coin is, "Your needs and wants are just as important as mine".

- **Tip 92** Do everything in moderation. Instead of over indulging in eating, smoking, drinking and spending. Think of balance and moderation.

- **Tip 93** Make holidays, "Holy Days". Beware of excessive commercialism. Remind yourself of the true meaning of Christmas and how to re-connect with God and your neighbor (family, friends, acquaintances, etc.)

- **Tip 94** Create and give meaningful gifts that touch the heart but cost less. One of my favorite gifts is a collage of pictures framed of my dad called, "...tell me bout the good ol' days".

- **Tip 95** Watch out for the $ugar Daddy or $ugar Mama syndrome. It takes an average of four months to pay off stress induced holiday bills. Figure out how much you can spend and pay only with cash. When the cash is gone you're done!

- **Tip 96** Spend time with the people YOU want to spend time with. Limit time with known "negaholics" and seek out the people that you want to bless and the people that bless you!

- **Tip 97** Tickle your funny bone plenty during the Ha Ha days!

When I was a high school freshman and stuck at the bottom of the tennis ladder, my coach, Jerry Slayton, inspired me with these words: "It's not your aptitude that determines your altitude, it's your attitude." I quickly responded, "I can have an attitude!" After 26 years of competitive tennis I have learned that attitude is what transforms underdogs into top dogs.

As I began climbing the ladder toward my master's degree in counseling psychology, this common-sense quote was further understood in the context of IQ versus EQ. IQ (Intelligence Quotient) is your aptitude. EQ (Emotional Quotient) is your attitude. Success is your altitude.

Researchers say that 70-80 percent of success is due to a person's emotional intelligence.

Men, you may not want to read this, but your emotional intelligence is more crucial than your intellectual knowledge. Most females have a head start on us because they were socialized to develop their emotional intelligence sooner than we were.

What would your family, friends, and co-workers say about your emotional intelligence?

Emotional intelligence can be divided into five major categories:

- **Tip 98** Knowing your own emotional world. This is your self-awareness and the ability to identify and label your feelings.

- **Tip 99** Managing your emotions. This is the ability to balance between the two extremes of stuffing feelings and spewing feelings.

- **Tip 100** Motivating your self. Jimmy Conners said, "The will to win is inside of you. You have to bring it out."

- **Tip 101** Recognizing emotions in others. How well can you read other people's body language and emotions?

- **Tip 102** Handling relationships. Brian Tracy says, "Eighty-five percent of success comes from relationships, 15 percent from achievements."

Game, set, match. If you want to play with confidence, serve others well, bounce back after any defeat, and always be a winner in everyday life, then keep climbing the ladder of emotional intelligence.

Life is a dance with others and we need the balance two step.

**Tips 98-102
EQ is more
important
than IQ.**

ON BALANCE:

- Personal balance leans on a variety of support.
- Personal balance deals with holiday stress.
- Personal balance utilizes emotional intelligence.
- Personal balance is all about handling relationships.

WHAT'S IN IT FOR ME?

_____

_____

_____

_____

_____

Chapter 8: The Balance Driven Life

When I was stuck at the top of that ladder for an hour, what do you think I spent my time doing? You're right — I was praying!

Not a day goes by that I do not remind myself of my roots, my foundation, my security, and my need for spiritual balance. The balance driven life includes spiritual balance.

It doesn't take a scientist to believe in God and know that we need Him. Early in my childhood my grandmother taught me about God. She taught me that I needed God and that God was true, unconditional love.

My heart has always had a vacuum for God. I was the little boy walking up to the altar at church and pulling on the preacher's pant leg at the end of the service.

In my teen years a loving Christian family with five sisters asked me to church. I went and was taught the basics of God. The church helped build my spiritual foundation, and I became a spiritual zealot. I was such a fanatic that my parents called my pastor and had a family meeting. They complained to him that I was out of balance with my spirituality and had a self-righteous attitude.

I felt called into church ministry and at age 18 began preaching. In college. People didn't know what to make of a guy who prayed four hours a day, read the Bible all the way through four times a year, and played on the tennis team with a cross painted on the strings of his tennis racquet.

After completing my bachelor's degree in sociology, psychology, and communications, I served as a youth pastor, then as the senior pastor of two churches, both of which asked me to leave because of my over zealousness.

BLESSED ARE THE BALANCED

Do you see a pattern? Do you think I was spiritually out of balance? What I needed to learn was, "Blessed are the balanced, for they shall beat burnout."

What is the foundation of your happiness, meaning, and balance? What is the foundation of your self-concept, self-esteem, and self-confidence?

Albert Einstein once said, "Everyone who is seriously involved in the pursuit of science becomes convinced that a Spirit is manifest in the Laws of the Universe — a Spirit vastly superior to that of man, and one in the face of which we, with our modest powers, must feel humble."

A day does not go by in the safety of my counseling office that a client struggling with these issues doesn't ask for my answer. As a professional counselor I do not force my values on others, though I do encourage people to explore their spiritual beliefs and their concept of God, and to develop spiritual balance.

One of my favorite scriptures that teaches spiritual balance is by King Solomon in Ecclesiastes 7:15-18, in the New International Version:

> "In this meaningless life of mine I have seen both of these: a righteous man perishing in his righteousness, and a wicked man living long in his wickedness. Do not be over righteous, neither be over wise — why destroy yourself? Do

not be over wicked, and do not be a fool — why die before your time? It is good to grasp the one and not let go of the other. The man who fears God will avoid all extremes."

Here are four tips to balance the scales of your spiritual connection.

- **Tip 103 Develop your concept of God as the ultimate and superior source of happiness, meaning, self-confidence, and balance.** This is difficult for people who compare God consciously or unconsciously to their earthly father figure.

Tips 103-106 Let go and let God.

- **Tip 104 Life is meaningless and chaotic without a foundation and relationship with God.** God is the center that gives balance to the edges of your life.

- **Tip 105 Humble yourself daily by admitting your need for God.** Trust God for power to live a balanced and healthy life. Repeat the old saying, "I know there is a God, and I'm not HIM."

- **Tip 106 Practice regular spiritual workouts.** Building and maintaining a spiritual connection is a discipline like exercise. Read, meditate, pray, worship, give, share your story, etc.

WHAT DO PENNIES, LADY BUGS AND NAILS HAVE IN COMMON?

In my morning quiet times I've been reading a book by Laurie Beth Jones entitled, "Jesus Life Coach." She tells a story of when she was a little girl struggling with rejection and feeling unloved. She loved ladybugs and told God if He really loved her to please send a ladybug. At that moment a ladybug landed on her arm. She continued sharing how the ladybug became a tangible sign of God's love for her in difficult situations. Even in one winter when she was stranded in a blizzard she prayed for God's help and love and a ladybug blew into her coat.

Laurie also shared of a friend of hers who believed every time he found a penny it was God showing in a visible tangible way that he was thinking of him and loved him.

Being inspired by these stories I started praying for a visible sign that God could secretly (I guess it's not secret now) show me his love. After one of my counseling sessions I was renewing my spirit, getting some sunshine, and walking around the block. I was talking with God and asked for some sign that He loved me. At that moment I looked down on the ground and there was a nail. I picked it up and excitedly said, "Yeah that's it!" Jesus demonstrated his love by being nailed to the cross. Every time I find a nail that is my secret sign from God. I continued walking and within minutes I found another nail that was totally different from the first. Finally, I was about to enter my outer office door and there was again another totally different nail. Three unique nails in a matter of ten minutes. Wow! I'm thinking Father, Son, and Holy Spirit. Now I have a jar that I'm placing all the nails in that I found to remind me of how much God loves me.

You may be thinking this spiritual experience is silly, but in psychological terms I had a peak experience! I felt connected with God, connected with my self, and connected with the world around me.

One of my clients who heard my story of the nails thought inside how silly and ridiculous this story was. He left my office and was walking to his truck when he looked down and there was a rusted nail. My client told me later that he kept that nail and took it as a sign from God to open up his spiritual mind.

Three weeks from my first nail experience, I was walking (again to keep the balance) and was feeling frustrated, alone, and bent out of shape. I was walking and talking with God when I looked down and there was a bent nail. I felt like God was telling me that he loves me even when I'm bent out of shape.

Do you feel rejected, unloved, or bent out of shape? Do you take time to balance your physical, mental, social, and spiritual life? What could be your secret sign between you and God that demonstrates His love?

Now you know what ladybugs, pennies, and nails have in common.

— Find your visible sign that God demonstrates his love.

Would you like to rise above all your earthly troubles? There's more than one way to do it.

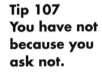

Tip 107
You have not because you ask not.

My parents gave my wife and me a ride in a hot air balloon for our birthdays last year. Finally, after four failed attempts, my wife and I were able to lift off some 1,500 feet above our problems and stresses. God knew just the right time when we needed to rise in the sky like a soaring eagle.

On May 12, 2006, Airventure Balloons gave us the ride of our lives in a 120,000-cubic-foot hot air balloon named The Winter Solstice. We were amazed at how rip-stop nylon the size of three football fields could be inflated with air heated with propane burners. As we jumped into the basket and the balloon began to rise, our eyes gained a new perspective on life.

The peaceful ascent was combined with blasts of heat that filled the balloon with hot air. For an hour, we drifted with the wind – approximately 30 miles. Interestingly, in ballooning you don't know where you're going to land, so wherever the wind takes you, you have to find a safe place to land. Our pilot made sure the balloon was safely away from power lines, trees, crops, cattle, etc., and we gently floated over a corral of horses before landing in a field behind two houses. It was an amazing adventure.

Since I'm full of hot air, let me share three quick tips about rising above your earthly problems.

**Tips 108-110
Let God arise
in your life.**

- **Tip 108 Find life's natural highs**. So many people try to escape their problems by getting high on illegal or unhealthy things. Take a risk, have an adventure, and experience life's natural highs.

- **Tip 109 Trust your pilot.** Who is your pilot in life? What are your spiritual beliefs? How do you build your trust in a pilot? We can have a spiritual pilot through God, and we can have earthly pilots that help guide us.

- **Tip 110 Land in a safe place.** It's true that we don't know where life will take us. Life is full of perils, sickness, and dangers. Each of us is responsible to land in a safe place. Who are the family members, the friends, the people, the places that are safe for you?

As I stood at the top of my ladder buzzing off tree limbs, I was nervously aware of how much balance I needed. In my mind, I battled to think positive thoughts. I felt both unpleasant and pleasant feelings as the wind swirled in my face. I forced myself to the top of the ladder even though I was thinking, "You're crazy." It was an adventure to go 45 feet in the air.

Do you want to climb the ladder of success without getting rung out? To clear the air for more sunlight in your life, keep seeking the balance driven life.

ON BALANCE:

- Spiritual balance helps when you are stuck in life.
- Spiritual balance is a journey.
- Spiritual balance requires spiritual workouts.
- Spiritual balance provides a pilot to help you land in a safe place.

WHAT'S IN IT FOR ME?

_____

_____

_____

_____

_____

SECTION III:

PROFESSIONAL BALANCE

Chapter 9: Take This Job and Love It!

Work keeps at bay three great evils: boredom, vice, and need.
                                        –Voltaire in *Candide*

Do you find meaning in your work? A 55 year old friend of mine who works at a coffee factory often complains that his work has no meaning. His attitude is, "take this job and shove it." He tells me that he does not make a difference in the world like I do as an author, counselor, coach, and speaker. My friend needs to learn how to take his job and love it.

I shared with my friend that he makes more of a difference in his work than he realizes. What would the world be like if people did NOT get their coffee?! I have heard many positive compliments about my friend in our little community how he is valued and makes a difference in people's lives.

Finding your purpose in work is important. However we must also realize that work will have it's own stress and frustrations.

**Tip 111
Let off some
steam.**

—Identify and rank your top three job frustrations.

___ Not enough money

___ Too many hours

___ Dead-end career

___ Too much paperwork

___ Not enough training

___ Not appreciated

___ Feeling powerless

___ Negative office politics

___ Sexism in the workplace

___ Poor public image

___ Conflicts with peers

___ Too much red tape

___ Conflict with boss

___ Other _____

___ Other_____

My informal survey sent to more than 1,000 people on my e-mail newsletter produced the following results.

The No. 3 frustration: Not enough money and not enough training

The best way to make more money is to increase your education and training, present a professional image, make yourself indispensable, and negotiate for more money. Research shows that more than $6 billion is spent on training in North America each year. Resources are available for more quality training. Employees, supervisors, the HR team, and the CEO need to realize the necessity of continuously sharpening the saw.

**Tip 112
Learn
to earn.**

— E-mail Brent O'Bannon at brent@brentspeaks.com for consultation on training development in your organization.

The No. 2 frustration: Feeling unappreciated

Sadly, many people don't get the appreciation they deserve. We all want and need genuine praise. In my opinion, employers often appreciate good workers but do a poor job in communicating that appreciation. Outside of work, it's easy to drop the ball and not communicate appreciation to parents, a significant other, children, and friends.

— Take time this week to write a note, give a card, send some flowers, and express creative appreciation.

Tip 113 Express appreciation.

The No. 1 frustration: Dead-end career

I'm amazed at how many people remain tied to an empty career with an invisible chain. You should ask yourself three questions: Do I truly understand how I can make a difference in the world with my work? Am I in a career that matches my aptitudes and passion? What keeps me from spreading my wings to fly toward a meaningful career?

— Go to the local community college or career testing center and do some career testing and planning.

Tip 114 Work to live.

Ninety-one percent of singles surveyed on match.com said they would rather fall in love with someone who was moderately successful and had a balanced life than a person who was very successful and a workaholic.

It appears this research supports the (slightly modified) adage, "All work and no play makes Jack a rich, but dull, boy."

Workaholics tend to work too much, avoid vacations, take work home, have few if any close relationships, and play or laugh little to none. Could it be that most workplaces take advantage of the workaholic? Could it be that most significant others hate to live with the workaholic?

Psychologists report there are at least two kinds of workaholics.

 1. The job-involved workaholic. This person feels "called" to a job or career and totally enjoys the

work. He is likely to be highly satisfied with both his work and life.

2. The compulsive workaholic. This person has lost control and is "addicted" to work. He tends to be rigid with himself, his co-workers, and his family. This type of workaholic has a high tendency towards burnout.

Work balance is not just the responsibility of the individual employee but of the workplace. Upper management needs to walk the talk of work/life balance. Research exposes 11 workplace factors that cause burnout.

Tips 115-125 Clean up corporate culture.

- **Tip 115 Ambiguity:** The priorities, rules, and expectations are constantly changing.

- **Tip 116 Alienation:** I'm isolated and don't have much in common with my co-workers.

- **Tip 117 Boredom:** My work is routine with little challenge, and I'm overqualified.

- **Tip 118 Conflict:** I disagree with people at work and I'm caught in the cross fire.

- **Tip 119 Inadequate information:** I'm left out of the loop and need more information.

- **Tip 120 Poor feedback:** I'm not sure if my work is right/wrong, good/bad, or acceptable.

- **Tip 121 Powerlessness:** I'm trapped with little control, and can't change the outcome.

- **Tip 122 Poor teamwork:** Office politics, poor cooperation, and favoritism.

- **Tip 123 Punishment**: I get blamed, the workplace is critical, and I'm unappreciated.

- **Tip 124 Unrewarding:** I have few successes, I'm not satisfied. This is a dead end job.

- **Tip 125 Value conflict:** I don't like my work and I have to compromise my values.

— Does your workplace value and encourage work/life balance? How could balance matter more in your workplace?

Tip 126 Discuss these workplace factors with your work team.

Brent's top 10 tips for a balance-friendly workplace:

- **Tip 127 Flextime** Can you alter your work schedule to attend your child's activities, take care of personal business, or take your aging parent to the doctor?

Tips 127-136 Don't live to work.

- **Tip 128 Telecommuting** Will your workplace allow you to work from your home PC and the Internet?

- **Tip 129 Child care** Does your workplace offer child care services? Does it provide child care spending accounts that give tax benefits ?

- **Tip 130 Elder care** Many baby boomers take care of their children as well as their aging parents. Is your workplace flexible when it comes to your elder care responsibilities?

- **Tip 131 In house store/services** Many companies committed to work/life balance have convenience stores with a pharmacy, dry cleaner, tailor, jewelry repair, shoe repair, and hair salon.

- **Tip 132 Paternity leave** With the passing of the Family and Medical Leave Act, companies can allow workers time off to care for children, elders, family emergencies, etc.

- **Tip 133 Education and training** Does your company invest in and promote learning opportunities?

- **Tip 134 EAP (Employee Assistance Program)** Do you take advantage of the free benefits offered through your company EAP? Check with your HR department for the 800 number, and discover all the resources available.

- **Tip 135 Wellness center** Many companies have a gym on site or offer a discount to a health club. Are you taking advantage of this opportunity?

- **Tip 136 Fun-loving corporate culture** Does your business promote playfulness, humor, and laughter?

WHAT IS STRESS?

Stress is simply wear and tear on your brain and body. Stress happens to all of us. Just as you maintain your car because of wear and tear, you must do maintenance on your life, too.

Have you longed for that new home that would be your perfect paradise? Nine years ago my wife, two kids and I moved into our lovely new hacienda. I assumed it would remain pristine forever. Recently, I began to notice the wear and tear of an active family: carpet stains, cracks in the marble floor, chipped paint, loose cabinet knobs, and toilet seats that needed replacing.

Active living causes wear and tear on a house, so imagine what it can do to your body and brain!

If you've been working, playing, and just plain living, you will experience stress. Don't assume your life will remain in a pristine condition.

My mother, who's in the process of moving from Florida to Texas, is changing homes, changing doctors, changing friends, changing routines, changing churches, and unfortunately, changing scenery.

"It's another beautiful day in paradise," she used to tell me by phone from scenic Destin, Florida. Sometimes we choose change, and sometimes change chooses us.

- **Tip 137 List the changes you are facing.** We feel frustration when we are blocked from reaching our goals. When a new mortgage company agreed to pay my property taxes then failed to do so, my frustration was evident.

Tips 137-140 Stress less.

- **Tip 138 List your frustrations.** Conflict can be internal or external. A recovering alcoholic battles the addicted side that wants to drink and the recovery side that wants to be sober. When parents want a child to finish her homework, she may talk back. If you want more creative technique's and skills in dealing with conflict, stay tuned for Brent's soon coming book, *Balance Matters in Conflict.*

- **Tip 139 List the conflicts you are ignoring or battling.** The expectations and demands placed on a person cause pressure. Many people struggle with self-imposed pressure to be the perfect housekeeper, perfect parent, or perfect child. Others have guilt trips about making more sales, "increasing the numbers," or making better grades.

- **Tip 140 List your top pressures.** Just because your home has a few stains, cracks, and loose knobs doesn't mean you have to bulldoze it. Same goes with your life. Instead of "self-destructing," identify your top pressures, take steps to make repairs, and enjoy the spiffed-up you.

BRENT'S TOP 20 STRESS BUSTERS

**Tips 141-160
Stress Busters**

- **Tip 141 Let yourself experience those uncomfortable feelings.** All growth requires change; all change is unsettling. Asking your boss for a raise is a risk – she may say no – but without risk, there is no progress.

- **Tip 142 Picture yourself in top form.** If you have to make a presentation, imagine yourself relaxed, successfully answering everyone's questions, feeling proud of your self for a job well done. Going to a scary party? See yourself arriving poised, calm, and self-possessed.

- **Tip 143 Talk back to the mirror.** Take 3 minutes before you turn in each night to look yourself in the eye and review out loud what you did that day that you are proud of. Try if for at least 60 days; you'll be amazed at the results.

- **Tip 144 Create a victory wall.** Frame and hang diplomas, certificates, and that snapshot of yourself crossing the finish line. Openly focusing on your strengths is a great way to get an ego boost.

- **Tip 145 Adopt an attitude that says gratitude.** Thank people who help you. They may help you again!

- **Tip 146 Go for it.** Even when you make a mistake, you learn something, which puts you that much closer to success. Don't get bogged down second-guessing yourself.

- **Tip 147 Ask for strokes.** When you need a pat on the back, speak up: "Honey, come see the great job I did cleaning up the garage," or "Was that a great dinner, or what?"

- **Tip 148 Make bedtime happy time.** Be careful about what you watch, listen to, and read before you settle in at night.

Research shows that when we're asleep, we're six times more likely to focus on what we were thinking about during the last 45 minutes before dozing off. Trade in the 10 o'clock news for a serene, inspirational book.

- **Tip 149 Give praise.** You'll make others feel good, and they'll want to do the same for you.

- **Tip 150 If you think it, ink it.** Write down your personal goals on index cards, one per card. Review them each morning for inspiration.

- **Tip 151 Talk yourself up.** We're constantly giving ourselves hurtful messages. Next time you put yourself down, replace the negative with a positive. Instead of "What a stupid thing to do," how about, "Good job trying."

- **Tip 152 Renegotiate any broken agreements.** When you don't do what you promise you'll do, you don't feel like a person of integrity. Apologize, and then rework or cancel the original agreement. "I know I told you I'd write that letter, but I don't have time. I'm sorry."

- **Tip 153 Say it isn't so.** When others judge you harshly, be quick to tell yourself, "No matter how you treat me, I'm still a worthwhile person." No one can make you feel inferior without your consent.

- **Tip 154 Ask for affection, and give it.** Virginia Satir, a respected family therapist, has said we need four hugs a day for survival, eight a day to maintain emotional health, and 12 a day for growth.

- **Tip 155 Create calm.** We all have an inner voice that can guide us, but we need to schedule quiet time each day to hear it. Go for a walk, take a leisurely bath, or meditate.

- **Tip 156 Adjust your outlook.** Understand that E + R = O: Events + Response = Outcome. You may not be able to change what happens to you, but you can control how you're going to feel about it. If you lose your job, how you regard that loss will determine whether you sit home depressed or move on.

- **Tip 157 Act "as if."** What would you do if you were promoted? What kinds of projects would you start? Who would you have lunch with? How would you dress? Do it now!

- **Tip 158 Start your own warm-and-fuzzy file.** Include a rundown of your achievements, big and small. Create a list of 50 good things about yourself. Put in notes you've received that compliment or congratulate you. Read through the file often, and update it regularly.

- **Tip 159 Simplify.** Fix or throw out anything that doesn't work. Get rid of old clothes, balance your checkbook, and clean out your office, garage, or attic. Remember, finishing what you start frees up your life.

- **Tip 160 Don't give up.** Jack Canfield's Chicken Soup for the Soul was rejected by 133 publishers before being accepted. This collection of stories offering inspiring life lessons has since spawned 32 additional "Chicken Soup" titles, which collectively have sold 30 million copies.

MAKE SENSE OF STRESS

Most of us are on the fast track, like the Indy 500. It's time we put the race car in park and take time to smell the roses (not to mention hear the birds, see the sky, stroke a cat's fur, and taste a freshly baked pie). Use your senses!

— Use your five senses to make sense of life.

**Tips 161-165
Live with all
your senses.**

- **Tip 161 Taste:** Slow down, enjoy your food, and savor the flavor. What's your comfort food?

- **Tip 162 Touch:** We all have self-soothing behaviors. Take and give longer hugs. What are ways to get your touch needs met?

- **Tip 163 See:** Take time to notice the details of nature. Look deeply into people's eyes. What are your favorite visual images?

- **Tip 164 Smell:** Take time to smell flowers, candles, fresh food, perfume, etc. What are your favorite smells?

- **Tip 165 Hear:** Listen closely to music, nature sounds, people's voices, etc. What are your favorite sounds? Live life with all of your senses, and you will make sense of life. Be sensual!

TIME MANAGEMENT LEADS TO A BALANCED LIFE

The key is not to prioritize what's on your schedule, but to schedule your priorities.

Remember: **TIME** stands for
To Increase My Efficiency.

Tips 166-215
Try these
"nifty 50"
time-saving
tips.

HOW TO DEAL WITH PAPER:

- **Tip 166 Scan it.**
- **Tip 167 Prioritize.**
- **Tip 168 File it.**
- **Tip 169 Shred it.**
- **Tip 170 Don't pile it.**
- **Tip 171 T-toss it.**
- **Tip 172 R-refer it.**
- **Tip 173 A-act on it.**
- **Tip 174 S-store it.**
- **Tip 175 H-halt it.**

(TRASH acronym by Stephanie Winston)

HOW TO DEAL WITH THE TELEPHONE:

- **Tip 176 Decide if and when you will answer it.**
- **Tip 177 Have a receptionist screen calls.**
- **Tip 178 Return calls two times per day.**
- **Tip 179 Use e-mail to prevent telephone tag.**
- **Tip 180 Stand up while talking.**
- **Tip 181 Time limit each call.**
- **Tip 182 Outline the call (opening, body, and conclusion).**
- **Tip 183 Talk with a smile.**

HOW TO DEAL WITH VOICE MAIL:

- **Tip 184 Speak clearly, slowly, and concisely.**
- **Tip 185 Leave name and number at the beginning and end of the call.**
- **Tip 186 Respond in priority.**
- **Tip 187 Return all calls.**
- **Tip 188 Be positive/upbeat.**
- **Tip 189 Leave a call-back time.**
- **Tip 190 Leave your e-mail address.**
- **Tip 191 Leave enough information to help the other person make a decision.**
- **Tip 192 Update your voice mail message periodically.**
- **Tip 193 Add playfulness.**

HOW TO DEAL WITH E-MAIL:

- **Tip 194 Read it, file it, or delete it.**
- **Tip 195 Don't let it pile.**
- **Tip 196 Read/respond two times daily.**
- **Tip 197 Use the 2-minute rule: If it can be taken care of in 2 minutes, do it.**
- **Tip 198 Use flag features.**
- **Tip 199 Use action folders.**
- **Tip 200 Proofread and spell check.**
- **Tip 201 Beware of forward features — it can end up at your boss's desk.**
- **Tip 202 Use cc and bcc wisely.**
- **Tip 203 Don't forward chain letters or jokes, unless asked.**

- **Tip 204 Don't write in anger.**
- **Tip 205 Never send a message you wouldn't want.**

HOW TO DEAL WITH MEETINGS:

- **Tip 206 Get input before scheduling a meeting.**
- **Tip 207 Invite only those who need to be there.**
- **Tip 208 Set the agenda with time frames.**
- **Tip 209 Send out an agenda and stick to it.**
- **Tip 210 Communicate the result or accomplishment desired/met in the meeting.**
- **Tip 211 Overview minutes from last meeting.**
- **Tip 212 Clarify members' responsibilities.**
- **Tip 213 Cover the most important items first.**
- **Tip 214 Cancel unnecessary meetings.**
- **Tip 215 Start on time (even if one person is missing) and end on time.**

ON BALANCE:

- Work is a way to make a difference in the world.
- The work place needs to be balance friendly.
- There are four major types of stress.
- Use the five senses to make sense of stress.
- Time management is effectiveness and efficiency.

WHAT'S IN IT FOR ME?

_____

_____

_____

_____

_____

Chapter 10: Professionals Lead with Es

As a novice tennis player at age 15, I was excited when my father took me to watch my first professional tennis tournament in Dallas. John McEnroe and Johan Kriek blasted serves, returns, and winners all over the court. I was amazed at how effortless and easy they made the game look.

You would probably agree with me that true professionals, no matter their craft, make their work look easy. Their work looks effortless because they are leaders and have learned to "lead with Es."

Would you like to achieve true professionalism and learn to lead with Es? Let's take a look at the first E, which is education.

EDUCATION

Have you ever been without a job and not knowing what's next? That was me in 1990. My wife and I argued about my decision to go back to school and work on my masters' degree in counseling psychology. We had two children to feed, and she was afraid the cost was too much and that getting a masters' really wouldn't pay off in the long run. Fifteen years later, my wife, family, and in-laws are glad I paid the price to further my education. Now, I practice as a Licensed Professional Counselor in the state of Texas.

Knowledge is power—and added income, too. The U.S. Department of Labor reports that holders of bachelor degrees earn 68 percent more and that those with masters' degrees earn, on average, 90 percent more than do people with only a high school diploma.

It's been said there are three levels of learning and knowledge: first you gain information, then practice the information and, finally, teach the information.

A formal education is a place to start, but not the place to stop. Professionals continue to learn by reading, attending workshops, asking questions, watching videos, having a mentor, and listening to audio programs. There are literally thousands of ways to learn in the School of Hard Knocks.

Tip 216
They that read will lead.

— Read a book you have been putting off.

Tip 217
They that listen will glisten.

— Listen to an audio program in your car.

Tiger Woods is the ultimate professional. Even though he is possibly the best golfer of all time, he continues to strive to learn more about the game by opening his mind to other teachers and coaches. If you want to drive your career to further success and finesse your way to the top of the leader board, start with education, continue with a learning spirit, and never close your mind to additional knowledge.

EXPERIENCE

What separates the men from the boys? What divides the old from the young? What distinguishes a professional from a novice? In that-all important job interview you will most likely hear the question, "What experience do you have?"

— Now's the time to update your resume or professional narrative.

**Tip 218
Review your experiences.**

Seventeen years ago, when I was 24 and a novice therapist, you might say I was armed and dangerous: armed with a master's degree and somewhat dangerous because I had very little experience. I felt unsure of myself. What do I say? How do I handle those complex problems? Older couples would come to counseling and give me a strange look that said, "Are you old enough to be counseling us?"

Some professions require you to have practicum or supervised experience before going out on your own. To be your best, you must gain a variety of experiences along the professional path.

Here's what Rick Warren wrote in the chapter "Employing Your Experiences" in his bestselling book, *The Purpose Driven Life*:

"You have been shaped by your experiences in life, most of which were beyond your control. God allowed them for his purpose of molding you. In determining your shape for serving God, you should examine at least six kinds of experiences from your past."

Family experiences: What did you learn growing up in your family?

_____

_____

Educational experiences: What were your favorite subjects in school?

_____

_____

Vocational experiences: What jobs have you been most effective in and enjoyed the most?

_____

_____

Spiritual experiences: What have been your most meaningful times with God?

_____

_____

Ministry experiences: How have you served God in the past?

_____

_____

Painful experiences: What problem, hurts, thorns, and trials have you learned from?

_____

_____

It is this last category, painful experiences, that God uses the most to prepare you for ministry. God never wastes a hurt! In fact, your greatest ministry will most likely come out of your greatest hurt. Who could better minister to the parents of a Down syndrome child than another couple who have a child afflicted in the same way? Who could better help an alcoholic recover than someone who fought that demon and found freedom? Who could better comfort a wife whose husband has left her for an affair than a woman who went through the agony herself?

God intentionally allows you to go through painful experiences to equip you for ministry to others. The Bible says, 'He comforts us in all our troubles so that we can comfort others. When others are troubled, we will be able to give them the same comfort God has given us.'

If you really desire to be used by God, you must understand a powerful truth: The very experiences that you have resented or regretted most in life — the ones you've wanted to hide and forget — are the experiences God wants to use to help others. They are your ministry!

For God to use your painful experiences, you must be willing to share them. You have to stop covering them up, and you must honestly admit your faults, failures, and fears. Doing this will probably be your most effective ministry. People are always more encouraged when we share how God's grace helped us in weakness than when we brag about our strengths."

WHY I GOT INTO COUNSELING

Many people ask me why I got into counseling. I had been rejected by two churches as their pastor and was facing a crisis in my marriage. I was never more ready for authentic healing. As I began a master's program in counseling psychology, I got honest with myself and entered counseling; with God's grace, my marriage, family, and peace of mind were saved. (You can read my professional narrative at www.brentspeaks.com.)

Tennis also gave me insights into important life lessons. It took years of tedious lessons, tiring practices, disheartening losses, angry blow-ups, and disillusioned dreams before I realized my dream of winning a state tennis title, playing collegiate tennis on a scholarship, and being part of a college team that was ranked 12th in the nation. But the ultimate for me was being ranked No. 1 in father/son doubles in Texas for two straight years. Becoming a true professional involved both winning *and* losing!

**Tip 219
Find your
racquet.**

— Jump into a new experience you have been dreaming about.

ENTHUSIASM

Why do so many more people enjoy college football than professional football? When asked that question, several of my friends unanimously replied, "College teams have enthusiasm!"

It's sad that many professionals have lost their enthusiasm. Not just football players, but doctors, teachers, accountants, salespeople, and a host of others.

Have you lost your enthusiasm for work? Would you like to work with Es? Learn today how to work with enthusiasm.

Norman Vincent Peale inspired his listeners when he said, "There is real magic in enthusiasm. It spells the difference between mediocrity and accomplishment."

Practice these tips to sprinkle the magic of enthusiasm into each day. You'll find that you will accomplish more.

Tips 220-222

• **Tip 220 Be the host to get the most!** Greet the day, your co-workers, and customers with intentionality. Instead of going through the motions, open the eyes of your heart with the same intention you greet your friends coming to your Christmas party.

• **Tip 221 Let it go and be gung ho!** Exaggerate your body language. Smile bigger, speak faster then slower, linger with the handshake, and make longer eye contact. Don't hold back, let it go and be gung ho!

- **Tip 222 Balance outstanding old with the novel new!** Reminiscing on the outstanding old in your life can create optimism, confidence, and celebration. Focusing on the "novel new" adds adventure and anticipation. Go ahead, play around with something old and something new.

Take it from Vince Lombardi, the greatest professional football coach: "If you aren't fired with enthusiasm, you will be fired with enthusiasm."

As Brent "The Balance Master" says, "Get fired up!"

EFFORT

How do you turn the tiger loose at work?

A few years ago Tiger Woods shot a record low score in a golf tournament. After the round he immediately went to a driving range where he worked until 10:30 p.m., when he was asked to leave.

True professionals work with Es. They work with education, experience, enthusiasm, and EFFORT!

An old proverb tells us that success is 99 percent perspiration. If we desire success we must be willing to pay the price. Part of that price is the effort of work and practice.

It's been said, "Winners are willing to do the things that losers are unwilling to do." You are a winner, so be willing to work with effort!

— Set up and follow a practice routine for one skill you want to improve.

**Tip 223
Practice,
practice,
practice.**

EXCELLENCE

When I was 2, my mother took a picture of me perfectly dressed in a black suit, white shirt, and tie. My hair was perfectly combed. She was communicating to me that "I should be perfect."

Like many of you, I struggle with perfectionism. Daily, I battle the evil thought that "I'm not good enough."

What is perfectionism? First, it's unrealistic expectations about yourself and others. Second, it's being overly concerned about small flaws in life, in yourself, and in others. Having perfectionism in the workplace will zap you of freedom, joy, success, and relationships.

Realize there is a difference between striving for excellence and striving for perfection. Excellence is your best. Perfection has no flaws. Working and living with excellence is attainable for everyone. Striving for perfection without mistakes is humanly impossible.

Tip 224
Forgive and let live.

— *Write a letter to yourself forgiving some mistake you have made.*

In my counseling office I have an antique table with some nicks in it. To me, those nicks give it character and beauty and make it one-of-a-kind.

Work with Es. Work with excellence. Give and go for your BEST!

Tip 225
Be positive.

— *Say this affirmation daily: "(Your Name)* _____, *is good, and good is good enough!"*

EXPERTISE

Would you like to work with Es? In this section you have learned about education, experience, enthusiasm, effort, and excellence. Next, I will help you develop your credibility power by building your expertise.

Whether you're a doctor, teacher, financial planner, speaker, or other professional, you should develop your own professional DNA. Differentiate yourself from others in your field by finding your niche. Take the time to discover your unique expertise.

We are familiar with such greats as Oprah Winfrey, Larry North, Martha Stewart, and Jack Canfield. But what about Michael Bohdan?

Michael is in the pest-control business. Yes, he kills cockroaches for a living. In 1985, Michael created the World's Largest Cockroach Contest. Soon afterward he wrote the book *What's Buggin' You?*; starred in his own radio show; was a guest on the *Tonight Show With Johnny Carson* (he has photos of Johnny walking a cockroach on a leash); and started the Cockroach Hall of Fame in his office.

If a man can parlay a knowledge of cockroaches into such fame, don't you think each of us can find a way to become a standout in our own field?

What is your educational background? What are your life experiences? What do you have enthusiasm for? What are your accomplishments? What do you excel in? Would you like the Balance Master, Brent O'Bannon, to help coach you in building your expertise?

— Read the book **Credibility Power: The Art of Selling Yourself** *by Richard Hansen, Allyn Dramer, and Larry Upshaw.*

**Tip 226
Niche to grow
rich.**

ENDURE

The all-time-great Jack Nicholas is a living legend. He is the ultimate professional golfer who has become immortal. Although Tiger Woods is the contemporary version of Jack Nicholas, Tiger knows he has to endure in his professional career to be compared to "The Golden Bear."

While you and I may never accomplish the feats of Tiger or Jack, we can become professionals who endure and leave an immortal legacy. In this last part of "Working with Es," I'll share the importance of endurance.

It's good to have a good thing going, and it's great to keep a good thing going. My hobbies of tennis and golf have taught me that to be successful, I must be consistent and endure hard times. Being a professional means working when you don't feel like working; it means enduring boredom, burnout, co-worker conflicts, disappointments, distractions, frustration, illness, and the tough times.

Tip 227
Endure to the end.

— *Write down what you must endure.*

Professional endurance is like running a marathon: you put one foot in front of the other and don't quit until you pass the finish line.

You need endurance in life, marriage, parenting, sports, and your profession. Even though you may feel like quitting, don't give up. Endure to the end, and you will develop an immortal legacy.

Always being professional means working with Es: education, experience, enthusiasm, effort, excellence, expertise, and endurance.

Professionals are leaders and we need to lead with Es.

ON BALANCE:

• Professionals are leaders and learners.
• Professionals use their experience to develop expertise.
• Professionals are enthusiastic and gung ho!
• Professionals strive for excellence with effort and endurance.

WHAT'S IN IT FOR ME?

_____

_____

_____

_____

_____

Chapter 11: Top 10 Winning Ways at Work

Winning within ourselves is the biggest battle any of us will ever face! Stephen Covey says, "Inner victories proceed outer victories." If you really want to be a winner then you must face the opponent within yourself. Winning is learning how to tame the tiger that lurks within. It's been said the difference between a champ and a chump is "U". Let's look at ten winning ways at work to the acronym **I AM A WINNER**.

I CAN ATTITUDE.

ACQUIRE RELAXATION SKILLS

MOTIVATION LEADS TO MENTAL TOUGHNESS.

ACCEPT PRESSURE AS A FRIEND.

WATCH YOUR HERO.

IMMERSE YOURSELF IN THE MOMENT

NEVER GIVE UP

NOTICE YOUR BODY LANGUAGE

EFFECTIVELY PRACTICE

REMEMBER TO ALWAYS HAVE FUN

I CAN ATTITUDE.

Believe you are a champion. Develop a positive optimistic attitude instead of a negative pessimistic attitude. A mother and her two teenage sons was attending counseling with me. One son was very negative, pessimistic, and struggled with an I can't attitude. The other son was very positive, optimistic, and excelled with an I can attitude. To help them discover a positive mindset, I asked them to look around my office and find three things that was positive. Of course the optimist raised his hand first. He identified one picture that had a man walking forward toward his goals. Then he commented on a picture with the ocean, which he stated there is always another side. For the third item he pointed to my clock and said there is always time to change. I turned to the second son and he said he could only come up with one positive in my office. The door. Do you see the difference between an I can attitude versus an I can't attitude?

Tips 228-238
Repeat winning affirmations

- **Tip 228 I am a winner.**
  (your name) _____ is a winner!
- **Tip 229 I am competent.**
  (your name) _____ is competent!
- **Tip 230 I am good enough.**
  (your name) _____ is good enough!
- **Tip 231 I am successful.**
  (your name) _____ is successful!
- **Tip 232 I am blessed.**
  (your name) _____ is blessed!
- **Tip 233 I am forgiven.**
  (your name) _____ is forgiven!
- **Tip 234 I am confident.**
  (your name) _____ is confident!

- **Tip 235 I am lovable.**
  (your name) _____ is lovable!
- **Tip 236 I am wealthy.**
  (your name) _____ is wealthy!
- **Tip 237 I am wise.**
  (your name) _____ is wise!
- **Tip 238 I am balanced.**
  (your name) _____ is balanced!

ACQUIRE RELAXATION SKILLS

When we become stressed we carry tension in our body. To perform our best we must practice relaxations skills. We have all seen the basketball player who is on the free throw line and has to make the shot to win the game in the final seconds. Notice that they shake their hands, bounce the ball, cleanse their thoughts, and focus on the goal for success. Any tension in their body could cause them to miss the free throw.

- **Tip 239 Squeeze each muscle, hold, now relax.**
- **Tip 240 Stretch each muscle group gently.**
- **Tip 241 Slowly shake the tension away from each muscle group.**
- **Tip 242 Take a deep breath through your nose. Fill up your lungs. Hold for five seconds. Now let out slowly through your mouth. Repeat several times.**
- **Tip 243 Breathe slowly and naturally from your diaphragm and not your chest. Breath in fully through your nose, exhale slowly through your mouth.**
- **Tip 244 Repeat and meditate on winning affirmations.**

Tips 239-244 Build your relaxation response

MOTIVATION LEADS TO MENTAL TOUGHNESS

Desire, motivation, and mental toughness come from the heart. In the movie, *The Guardian* Kevin Costner played a rescue swimmer with the Coast Guard. He saved many peoples lives. One story was how he pulled a man from a boat. The helicopter was pulling them up with a cable through the storm and Costner said, "I won't let go." He held on even though he dislocated his shoulder and tore tendons while holding on to the man. That is motivation and mental toughness. Jimmy Conners once said, "The Will to win is inside of you. You have to bring it out."

**Tip 245
Exercise
mental
toughness**
— *Each time you exercise go at least one more repetition than you think you can.*

ACCEPT PRESSURE AS A FRIEND

It is true that many people are afraid of pressure. They get nervous and fold under pressure. They have not learned to manage their stress. They may not see pressure as a friend. Pressure is an opportunity to help us perform at a higher level. One Christmas my wife and I were wrapping presents in front of the fire place. I found a doodle bug or sometimes called a Rolly Polly. It was the smallest rolly polly I had ever seen. As I placed it into my palm I noticed that it was stuck in a ball and would not open up. I gently placed a little pressure from my finger onto the bug. He opened up and began walking all over my arm. Sometimes we need a little pressure to help us open up to new possibilities. It is true that a diamond is a chunk of coal that was crystallized under pressure.

WATCH YOUR HERO

When I first started playing tennis as a young boy I wanted to play as good as Bjorn Borg and John McEnroe. When I went to my first tennis camp I learned a valuable lesson. It is important to watch your hero. We watched video tapes (that dates me) of the tennis legends. We learned by watching them play under pressure. The more you watch your hero the more you will perform like your hero. Everyone needs a hero to watch and learn from. Who is your hero? Do you have a hero for different areas of life?

—*Identify your personal heroes.*

Tip 246 Watch your heroes

_____

_____

—*Identify your professional heroes.*

_____

_____

IMMERSE YOURSELF IN THE MOMENT

It is so easy to get distracted by the outer annoyances in our environment. Do you know people who can stay focused, be in the moment, and block out all the distractions around them? This is a skill that can be developed. I loved the movie Gladiator. Every time Russel Crow was ready to fight he would kneel down pick up a handful of dirt, smell it, and immerse himself in the moment. We are not effective when we live only in the past or the future. We need to have a balance of the past, the future, while immersing ourselves in the present.

- **Tip 247 Do a Russel Crow imitation and smell the dirt.**

- **Tip 248 Look deeply into people's eyes when you talk to them.**

Tips 247-248 Be in the moment

Tips 249-250
Enjoy life

- **Tip 249 Stop and smell the flowers.**
- **Tip 250 Take a deep breath and remember you were meant to live your best.**

NEVER GIVE UP

When we live life we will make mistakes. Failure is optional. Failure is giving up. You may have heard the story of the little boy who showed his dad how great a home run hitter he was. He tossed his plastic ball up and swung with his plastic bat. He missed. He told his dad again, I am the world's greatest home run hitter. He tossed the ball, swung, and again he missed. Even more determined he told his dad he was the best batter in the world. He tossed his ball, swung a third time, and again swoosh. He missed. The boy looked at his dad and said, "Like I said, I'm the world's greatest pitcher." It is true that sometimes in life we need to change our focus to what we excel at. That is not giving up. That is moving on. When I make a mistake in golf, I do my best when I remember to tell myself, "recovery." I most often make the next shot a great shot because I'm not giving up and focusing on recovery.

Tips 251-254
Don't give up,
move on

- **Tip 251 Repeat the affirmation-Recovery.**
- **Tip 252 Repeat the affirmation-Rebound.**
- **Tip 253 Repeat the affirmation-Bounce back.**
- **Tip 254 Repeat the affirmation-Keep playing.**

NOTICE YOUR BODY LANGUAGE

My high school tennis coach taught me the importance of body language on the court during a match. Many people droop their shoulders, sigh, shake their head in disgust, throw their racquet, hit a ball into the fence, or have a screaming fit. I must admit that I have no doubt done all of those sometime in my thirty years of tennis. When we are down or not performing our best we still need to have confident body language. That means holding our head up, making good eye contact, walking with purpose, controlling our emotions, and moving with a mission to give our winning best.

- **Tip 255 Give solid handshakes when you greet someone.**
- **Tip 256 Give balanced eye contact. Not too short, not too long.**
- **Tip 257 Walk with purpose. Not to fast, not too slow.**
- **Tip 258 Stand and sit erect with good posture.**
- **Tip 259 Take deep breaths to manage your emotions.**

Tips 255-259 Use confident body language

Effectively Practice

The great coach of Notre Dame, Joe Paterno said, "The will to win is worthless, with out the will to prepare." The greatest leaders, sports stars, and people in life are those who don't only rely on talent. They work consistently by practicing perfectly. Practice doesn't make perfect. Perfect practice makes perfect. We need to practice and polish anything we do that is to be great. In this context perfect is referring to excellence.

Tips 260-263
Perfect
practice
makes perfect

- **Tip 260 Practice like you play**
- **Tip 261 Practice your next speech, sell, proposal in front of the mirror.**
- **Tip 262 Practice assertive communication skills by writing and then rehearsing what you need to share with someone.**
- **Tip 263 Join a local Toastmasters group for communication and leadership practice. Go to www.toastmastersinternational.org to find your local club.**

REMEMBER TO ALWAYS HAVE FUN

Basketball coaching legend, John Wooden said, "Success is the peace of mind in knowing that you have done your best, to become the best, you are capable of becoming." We must remember that success is not just results but a process. Winning is learning to give our best while relaxing, laughing, making friends, and enjoying the journey. Get ready for the next two chapters on becoming forever playful.

Tip 264
Enjoy the
process

— Whether you win or loose focus on enjoying the process with a playful attitude.

ON BALANCE:

- Winning within our self is the biggest battle.
- Winners have internal and external confidence.
- Winners have to practice to get winning results.
- Winners are needed in the work place.

WHAT'S IN IT FOR ME?

_____

_____

_____

_____

_____

SECTION IV:

PLAYFUL BALANCE

Chapter 12: Lighten Up. I'm Serious!

Wipe that smile off your face. This is serious business. Act your age. Get serious! Who hasn't heard those some time in their life? Parents, teachers, churches, and workplaces often promote a terminally serious world. We grow up humor-deprived. We get stuck on the treadmill of seriousness, and life becomes monotonous.

Sure, the world has many serious problems. But as John McEnroe once said in a screaming fit to a tennis linesman: "You can't be serious!" That's what I'd like to scream to the world: You can't be serious! You can be serious-minded, professional, and playful at the same time. That's forever playful.

How do we lighten up and become more playful? How do we replace frowns with smiles and laugh lines? How do we become less focused on winning and losing and more enlightened about how we PLAY the game?

A teenager with a Mohawk, tattoos, and piercings attending his weekly counseling session brought a smile to my face when I read this on his black T-shirt: "I'm immature, unorganized, lazy, and loud, but I'm FUN!" Now that is a playful attitude.

Face it: Many of us adults have lost the spirit of having fun. Our T-shirt would likely read: "I'm mature, organized, industrious, assertive, and BORING."

Tip 265
Don't be a
"funsucker."
— Darren
LaCroix

— Buy and wear a T-shirt that sports a funny line.

People want to have fun. People need to have fun! Abraham Maslow, a psychologist who studied successful people, taught that all people have these needs: physical, safety, love, esteem, cognitive, pleasure, and self-actualization. Notice that humans have a need for pleasure. Pleasure is another word for fun, entertainment, laughter, and play.

Tip 266
Meet the
need.

— Get your needs met in a healthy way this week.

Here are four light-hearted tips to sweeten your personal and professional life.

1. Lighten up with a smile.

A smile is a curve that sets everything straight.

Phyllis Diller

Psychologist James Laird of Clark University discovered that frowns trigger painful memories and that smiles trigger happy memories. Go ahead, try it.

— *Try this: Frown with your entire face for 60 seconds. Notice your thoughts and feelings. Now relax and smile with your entire face for 60 seconds. Notice your thoughts and feelings.*

Tip 267
Smile big.

Congratulations, you have just exercised your zygomaticus muscles. (By the way, if your face felt tired after smiling, you probably need to smile more.)

2. **Smiling connects you to people.** It instantly shows acceptance, in all languages.

Antoine de Saint-Exupery was a fighter pilot captured in the Spanish Civil War. Locked behind bars, he was guarded by a vicious jailer who made no eye contact; Saint-Exupery feared for his life. As he fumbled for a cigarette that had been overlooked in a search, he peered through the bars at the jailer and asked, "Do you have a light?" As the jailer walked toward him, he made slight eye contact and Saint-Exupery nervously cracked a smile. The jailer smiled back, and an instant connection between two human hearts was formed. They began to talk about their children and marriages. Quietly, the guard unlocked the door and led the pilot to freedom. Saint-Exupery was amazed that his life had been saved by a smile.

I was driving to work recently in slow, backed-up traffic. I looked to my right and saw a guy beaming at me with a big cheesy smile. I could never figure out whether I knew the guy, but his smile made me smile for the rest of the day.

Tip 268
Smile, smile, smile.

— Smile at a perfect stranger today and see what happens.

3. Smiling changes your mood.

My 15-year-old son was learning to drive. Trent forgot to put on his seat belt, and I was giving him the seat belt lecture for the seven-billionth time when he beamed at me and said, "The magic of a smile." The little smarty-pants used my very own smile therapy against me — and it worked!

Tip 269
Smile in hard times.

— Smile at your family member the next time you are in an argument.

4. Smiling creates confidence.

In 2004, the world tuned in to watch the final round of The Masters. Phil Mickelson had played 47 major tournaments without a first-place finish. People doubted his abilities because he would get so close to winning but never close the deal. As I watched him play this final round, I noticed he was smiling. On hole number 18 he putted for a birdie to win his first major championship. Later in an interview Mickelson said, "I kept saying to myself: This is my day."

Never doubt that a smiling face can give you winning confidence!

Tip 270
Smile, you're on Candid Camera.

— Smile and say to yourself, "This is my day."

SELF-EFFACING HUMOR

How do angels fly? They take themselves lightly. We need to learn to lighten up with self-effacing humor.

In a workshop about snap judgments and first impressions, I asked members of the group how they would describe a psychotherapist. Without hesitation, one woman answered: "Crazy, psychotic, and a dysfunctional family."

I giggled and said, "Who told you my job qualifications?"

Many times, I am introduced at speaking engagements as the younger version of Dr. Phil. On my 40th birthday, my daughter gave me a card with a picture of Dr. Phil that said, "On your birthday, remember: YOU are in charge of your own life. YOU are in charge of your own happiness. YOU are in charge of your own gift."

Then my wife stood up, poked me on the chest and said, "Remember, I'm in charge of your MasterCard." "Yes, honey," I replied. "Like they say, men are from Mars; women are from VISA."

When I needed a letter of recommendation, my business associate yanked my chain when he wrote:

To Whom It May Concern:

Since I have known Brent O'Bannon for two years in a clinical capacity, it is important for me to say that the articles in the newspaper are false. The animal cruelty allegations could not be true because I know that during the alleged event, Brent was visiting his cousin Maynard in West Texas for the birth of Maynard's calf, which he felt was his very own.

The private-practice setting is well-suited for Brent since he must be in control of his business and money. In fact, he does not need an accountant since he keeps all his income in a jar under the couch.

Brent's clinical skills are well known. Not a week goes by that his name is not mentioned by the police, prominent judges, and the local courts.

Please give Brent due consideration — at least, more than the group at 20/20 did in their expose' last month.

Sincerely,

Bill Mory, Ed. S.

Taking yourself too seriously is a deadly disease. One of my clients helped put my deep psychological work into perspective when I asked what the counseling was doing for her. She said, "You're my garbage man." That cleaned things up!

When I was excited about making it the Toastmasters District Speech Contest out of 2,000 contestants, I called my mother-in-law to share the news and invite her to attend. She immediately put me in my place by saying, "I knew you had a mouth on you." In-laws have that special ability to make us feel the love!

One person who evaluated my workshop wrote: "A little cheesy, cliché, and sophomoric." Instantly I chuckled and thought of what my mother calls those things: "BS." See what a master's degree in counseling psychology gets you.

The late-night king of comedians is, of course, David Letterman. After a rift of 16 years with Oprah, he invited her to be on his show, and she accepted. He opened by saying, "Everyone is so excited about Oprah being on the show tonight. Even my mother said, 'She might switch over from Leno.' " By humbling himself with self-effacing humor, the big shot of comedy scored brownie points with me and many, many others.

An interesting study was done comparing two people interviewing for a job. They both had the same education, experience, abilities, and professionalism. The only difference was that in the interview one person spilled a cup of coffee. Who do you think was hired? The person who spilled the coffee, because the mishap showed his "human side." Poking fun at ourselves and using self-effacing humor is a safe way to share our human side. As someone brilliantly said, "People would rather hear about the time you fell on your face than the time you won a race." Face it: people like dirt. So lighten up, share your dirt, and stop taking yourself too seriously.

— Practice your self-effacing humor with family, friends, and co-workers.

**Tip 271
Take yourself
lightly.**

Lighten up with humor.

A well-developed sense of humor is the pole that adds balance to your steps as you walk the tightrope of life.

William Arthur Ward

Research reveals many benefits to having a humor mindset. They include:

PHYSICAL
Exercises muscles.
Increases relaxation.
Decreases pain levels.
Enhances immune system.
Reduces stress hormone levels.

PSYCHOLOGICAL
Buffers stress.
Reduces anxiety and feelings of helplessness.
Helps you through the hard times.
Helps you connect with others.
Increases self-esteem.

WORK
Enhances team-building.
Strengthens relationships.
Enhances creativity.
Increases employee morale.
Helps manage stress and conflicts.

**Tips 272-277
Be a humor
scientist.**

- **Tip 272 Make a list of TV sitcoms you have enjoyed over the past 10 years. What about them did you enjoy?**

- **Tip 273 What funny personal, family, or work stories are your favorites?**

- **Tip 274 Make a list of your favorite cartoons found in newspapers and magazines. Why do they make you laugh?**

- **Tip 275 Make a list of funny movies you have enjoyed over the past 10 years. What did you like best about them?**

- **Tip 276 List your favorite stand-up comedians. What do you like about their type of humor?**

- **Tip 277 Using the lists you've just made, name the things that make you laugh. Word play? Absurdities? Exaggerated everyday life events? Mannerisms?**

Are people born funny or must they learn how to be funny? I don't have the final word on funny, but I do believe we all have a genetic predisposition to be humorous, and we certainly have the potential to be more playful. Telling jokes is one way to be funny and playful. Since we all have a "joker" inside of us, I'd like to share some tips on telling jokes.

- **Tip 278 Choose jokes you think are funny.**

**Tips 278-284
Be a joker.**

- **Tip 279 Don't tell needless information about where you heard the joke.**

- **Tip 280 Personalize the joke by making it believable.**

- **Tip 281 Tell the joke without dragging it out. Get to the punch line ASAP!**

- **Tip 282 Do not laugh at your own joke, especially in advance.**

- **Tip 283 When joke-telling, animate your voice and body language.**

- **Tip 284 If people don't laugh, move on; don't make it worse by explaining the joke.**

Practice these 17 laugh tips by matching the examples A through Q to the laugh tips 285-301.

EXAMPLES

A. Where you can hang up tabloids, cartoons from the newspapers, funny pictures, etc.

B. You'll find a whole humor section in your favorite bookstore. Pick one or even two!

C. Play part of the tape another time for yourself, for family members, or associates.

D. Smiles help you look younger and make others wonder what you really know!

E. Lean over to turn on the bathtub faucet and get doused by the shower. Or, wait a half hour at the bakery before realizing you need to take a number.

F. Share your jokes with someone else.

G. "Enjoy life; this is not a dress rehearsal."

H. Popcorn to share with others.

I. Hang around with people who make you laugh.

J. Each day, when you tear off the page, leave it where others can see it, and write a note to a friend.

K. News flash! "How to lose 10 pounds a week eating chocolate," "3-week-old child has twins," etc.

L When you laugh at problems and inconsistencies, even though life may be unjust you're in control.

M. Teddy bear, stress ball, Slinky, yo-yo, train whistle, hand puppets, and bubbles.

N. Doodle or scribble. Be creative!

O. Read funny greeting cards!

P. Playing cards, board, and/or word games, puzzles.

Q. Play holiday music all year round. Try carousel music.

_____ **Tip 285 Smile more.**

_____ **Tip 286 Try to laugh at your problems more.**

_____ **Tip 287 Keep a funny, 365-page calendar in your kitchen or car.**

_____ **Tip 288 Use a fun poster, mug, button, T-shirt, and sign that say things like:**

_____ **Tip 289 Make a collection of toys and share them with co-workers, friends, and family. Toys help break the ice, inducing playfulness and laughter.**

_____ **Tip 290 Tape a late-night comedy show.**

_____ **Tip 291 Keep a box of crayons and blank paper handy.**

_____ **Tip 292 Listen to different music. Sing a lot.**

_____ **Tip 293 Keep a book of humor.**

_____ **Tip 294 Write down a joke you've heard, or tear one out from a magazine or paper.**

_____ **Tip 295 Have at least one "game" you can play.**

_____ **Tip 296 Spend a half hour each week in a gift store.**

_____ **Tip 297 Try to laugh at yourself and see the funny side of a situation, like when you:**

_____ **Tip 298 Collect and hang up the "best" of the tabloid newspapers.**

_____ **Tip 299 The next time you go to a meeting, bring**

_____ **Tip 300 Set up a "humor bulletin board."**

_____ **Tip 301 Be sensitive with whom you spend time.**

**Tips 285-301
Tickle your
inner clown.**

Answers, in reverse order: 301-I, 300-A, 299-H, 298-K, 297-E, 296-O, 295-P, 294-F, 293-B, 292-Q, 291-N, 290-C, 289-M, 288-G, 287-J, 286-L, 285-D.

LIGHTEN UP WITH LEISURE

Laughter is an instant vacation.
Milton Berle

A buddy had been traveling almost three weeks before finally getting a week off to relax. I was feeling stressed from parenting duties and missed hanging out with him. What a relief when he called the next Saturday morning and said, "Let's play Ping-Pong." Off we bounced to enjoy a playful game of Ping-Pong.

Tip 302
Play a game.
— *Play a game of Ping-Pong with someone you need to spend time with.*

Summer is the time for leisure, recreation, and vacations! What fun activities do you enjoy away from the daily grind?

One study in 1978 found that most men felt more satisfaction from leisure activities than from work. But in 1993, a study revealed that most Americans would rather work more hours and earn more money.

In counseling hundreds of people, I have discovered that many people who struggle with depression, anxiety, loneliness, anger, addictions, and a host of other issues don't make time for leisure, recreation, or vacations. Some never learned how to play as children, some are afraid of relationships, and some make the excuse that adults should not be frivolous. They're continually on the treadmill of seriousness.

Tips 303-307
Play pays.
— *Pick one leisure activity from each group to play in the next week.*

- **Tip 303 Hobbies** include playing music, singing, bird watching, gardening, knitting, collecting stamps, camping, fishing, hiking, restoring cars, etc.

- **Tip 304 Games** include chess, checkers, Scrabble, cards, dominoes, computer games, bridge, etc.

- **Tip 305 Travel** and vacations can be to far-away places such as the pyramids, to the nearest museum, or to Grandma's house.

- **Tip 306 Volunteer** activities could include working at a local hospital or nursing home; mentoring a young person; reading at a school; or giving time at church.

- **Tip 307 Sports** could include running, tennis, golf, scuba diving, dancing, bowling, softball, soccer, motorcycle riding — and the list goes on.

After 30 minutes of friendly chitchat, bursts of liberating laughter, and the challenge of almost winning left-handed, playing Ping-Pong produced connection, challenge, and creativity. Take time to balance your work life with plenty of leisure, and you will enjoy the last laugh.

ON BALANCE:

- Climb off the treadmill of seriousness.
- Lighten up with self-effacing humor.
- Nurture your inner clown by telling jokes and funny stories.
- Lighten up with play and leisure.

WHAT'S IN IT FOR ME?

_____

_____

_____

_____

_____

Chapter 13: Jump on the Trampoline of Playfulness

You can learn more about a person in one hour of play than a year of conversation.

Plato

After college I jumped into the rat race. I rarely smiled and, frankly, I became downright boring. It was only after seeing the movie *Patch Adams* that I was inspired to climb off the treadmill of seriousness and jump onto the trampoline of playfulness.

My opportunity to jump into play came one day when a single mother brought her two young daughters to a counseling session. The week before, I had told the girls they could bring any game they wanted and that I would play it with them. Their choice? Pretty Pretty Princess. That's right – Pretty Pretty Princess.

Before long, I was adorned with a tiara, jewelry, and a feather boa. The girls smiled and giggled as they paraded me through my crowded waiting room. You should have seen people's expressions. (That day I certainly redefined the title "psycho-therapist.") Yes, it was embarrassing, but it was so… worth it.

Knowing the children came from an abusive home and needed a father figure, I was happy that one hour of play brought happiness and healing like I have never seen. In fact, the power of play brought happiness and healing into my own heart!

**Tip 308
Make a child
laugh.**

— *Play a game with a child this week.*

"Play releases an individual from the past and ghostly voices and brings attention into the present. Fear and memories of past failures or hurts vanish because there is simply no room for them to exist in the present. There is a release from the bondage of the past wounds and a negative future is not anticipated. There simply is no time for past or future during the present of play. This peak experience is labeled as fun. Fun is the antidote to the ills of time and produces a unification of mind and body and creates full involvement. Fun is not trivial; it is essential. Contrary to the Puritan concept that life is suffering and acceptance of suffering is the goal, the purpose of life is cultivation of happiness. Life should be fun!" — from *The Need for Playing* by Gary Schwartz

CHILDLIKE PLAY

Don't be so full of adult there is no child in you.

Bob Basso

Another fun story of being playful and playing like a child came from one of my eZine readers.

Nicky shared that she and her 2-year-old daughter made Valentine cakes with an Easy-Bake Oven. They made the biggest mess not only in the kitchen but on each other, too. Cake batter in the hair, icing on the face, and the most beautiful 3-inch lopsided cake you had ever seen. Nicky said that experience was delicious, beautiful, and the most FUN she has had in years.

Don't be a fuddy-duddy! Remember, to have fun you don't have to be childish, just childlike!

Try these ideas:

- **Tip 309 Blow bubbles.**
- **Tip 310 Squirt a water gun.**
- **Tip 311 Color in a coloring book.**
- **Tip 312 Play hide and seek.**
- **Tip 313 Watch cartoons.**
- **Tip 314 Throw water balloons.**
- **Tip 315 Play hop scotch.**
- **Tip 316 Jump rope.**
- **Tip 317 Have a watermelon-eating contest.**

**Tips 309-317
Don't be a
fuddy-duddy.**

FUN TRADITIONS

My dad has a fun tradition. He and his high school buddies get together every year and go to the Texas State Fair. They love to play Flip a Chick, where you place a chicken on a catapult and bang the catapult with a mallet in an attempt to get the rubber chicken to land in a rotating skillet. My dad is the reigning Flip a Chick champion. He says he loves it because it takes absolutely no athletic ability.

— *Start a new fun tradition.*

**Tip 318
Start fresh
and new.**

While watching the TV show *The Bachelor*, I fell in love with a favorite quote of one of the bachelorettes. She said, "Work like you don't need the money, dance like no one is watching, and love like you have never been hurt."

Do you remember the complete joy, fun, and freedom you felt as a child dancing?

One of my clients shared how as a child her mother scolded her one day when she was caught dancing without inhibition and shaking her booty. After that, she became afraid, insecure, and ashamed of expressing herself. She lost her childlike playfulness.

As a teenager I danced without worrying what people thought. But as I got older, I began to fear looking like a fool on the dance floor. I have to admit, I'm not a good dancer, and my wife and daughter have reminded me of this many times. But when he gets a little encouragement, the little boy inside of me is not afraid to let loose and dance.

Dancing is a great way to have fun. Dancing is a playful exercise in leaping, laughing, and letting loose of all the seriousness we hold onto. My wife and I made a New Year's resolution to take a dance class together.

**Tip 319
Let loose.**

— *Take a dance class.*

Come on, people, get off your buns and find your dance partner. Live, laugh, and have fun by dancing like no one is watching!

**Tip 320
Get off your
buns.**

— *Dance tonight with your loved one.*

BLAST FROM THE PAST

Recently, I received a phone call that was a blast from the past.

I had just finished a counseling session when my office manager told me, "Someone is on the line waiting to talk with you." I picked up the phone and the female voice said, "FJPA. Does that ring a bell?" "No, who is this?" I asked. She answered with a question: "What kind of scientist were you when you were a kid?" A bell went off in my head. "Susan! Susan, is that you?" We then exploded in childlike giggles. (If you want to know what kind of scientist I was as a kid, you'll have to ask me personally.)

Susan and I started in the first grade together but have not seen each other in maybe 20 years. Her parents were best friends with my parents, so she was like a cousin. Our families would get together every week for some kind of fun activity.

Susan and her family now live in California. She decided to Google my name and found my Web site. The rest is history!

Susan e-mailed me after our phone conversation. "You didn't get the FJPA thing," she wrote. "That event is etched into my memory! Federal Junior Police Agents. We decided we were going to buy a CB radio to protect our neighborhood. We went door-to-door collecting money. Then I told my mom, and we had to return the money."

Oh yeah, now I remember!

Susan, her husband, and parents recently visited our home and had dinner with us. It was such a playful break in the week to visit, tell stories, laugh, and renew old friendships.

Is there someone from your past who you are curious about? Do you remember funny things you did as a child? Why not call that childhood friend and visit, tell stories, laugh, and add some playfulness to your daily grind?

— Call, visit, spend time with someone from your fun past.

**Tip 321
Rekindle
friendships**

HUMOR OF NICKNAMES

I was reminded of the humor of nicknames one recent Thanksgiving when I saw a 30-something cousin I had not seen in ages. I greeted her with, "Hi there, Pooky." She smiled ear to ear, slapped me on the back, and said, "I haven't heard that in years."

Sometimes there is a story behind a nickname, and sometimes it is just a silly name that brings fun and laughter. My nickname growing up was "Brentabeast." My wife's was "Robug." One man was affectionately nicknamed "Newman" when he became the "new man" at the company.

If you really want to have some fun with silly names, go to Professor Poopypants' Change-o-chart and get a new name. Mine is Lumpy Burgerchunks (since turning 40 I have felt a little like that). Find humor in a new moniker from *http://apps.scholastic.com/captainunderpants/NameGame/play.htm*. *Remember, the name should not bring someone down or hurt him.*

Tips 322-323
Get silly.

- **Tip 322 Share your nickname with a co-worker.**
- **Tip 323 Go to the Professor Poopypants Web site and get a new nickname.**

Stress was squeezing the life out of me. I was heavy from all the grown-up stuff like responsibility, money, and parenting. For my lunch break this day, I went to the park to play.

Yes, it is a little funny seeing a grown man in a business suit playing on the merry-go-round! I'm sure the people in the neighborhood watch had binoculars in one hand and were about to call 911 with the other.

On that afternoon, I was reminded how my inner child needed to be nurtured with some childlike play. After eating my lunch at the picnic table, off to the swing set I skipped (OK, I didn't skip, but I should have). As I soared in that swing, the stress began to loosen its grip. Then I scurried up the shiny slide and slid down with a silly grin on my face.

Lunch break over, both my inner child and "outer man" felt relaxed and happy.

Tips 324-327
Grin and bear it.

- **Tip 324 Go to the park during lunch this week.**
- **Tip 325 Swing on the swing set like a child.**

- **Tip 326 Slide down the slide with a silly grin.**
- **Tip 327 Ride the merry-go-round or a another ride.**

FAMILY PLAY

My best friend suggested we buy a Ping-Pong table as a Christmas present to each other. We set it up in my garage, and it's amazing how that that Ping-Pong table has helped a host of people to play.

Within two weeks, my son had taught his girlfriend how to play. It's a blessing when your teenager wants to stay home and play a game! A friend has bombarded me with voice mails, e-mails, and text messages asking when we will play our next Ping-Pong match. When he and his two sons join us, the CD player blares and the Ping-Pong balls fly. At the annual O'Bannon Christmas party, folks were sitting inside the garage and laughing at a game of "beer pong." (Don't worry, we played in excess yet drank in moderation.) My wife and daughter have even surprised us with their presence in the garage, showing off their athletic coordination.

The simple gift of a playful game of Ping-Pong has opened my home for friends and family to connect. Friendly conversation combines with aerobic exercise and belly laughs. Take time this week to play!

The truth of balance is not whether you win or lose, but IF you play the game.

When is the last time you, your significant other, your children, your extended family, or your friend's had fun?

JIMMY BUFFET CONCERT

You know Jimmy Buffet from his songs *Cheeseburger in Paradise* and *Margaritaville*. (Hey, what's stopping you from kicking back and having one or the other right now?) Are you surprised that Jimmy Buffet said, "If we didn't laugh we would all go insane!"

Thanks to my awesome dad, my wife and I had a "Parrothead" experience south of disorder at the Smirnoff Music Center in Dallas.

I knew that concerts can be a fun-filled experience, but wow! The tailgating was totally rollicking and frolicsome. I've never seen so much creative beach decorating in one parking lot: tiki huts, swimming pools filled with crawfish, karaoke bars, motorized coolers, Hula Hoop contests, and the best grilled food you've ever tasted.

To keep from "going insane" (and have a little fun), how about singing, dancing, and laughing with your favorite concert artist this summer? Why not? "It's 5 o'clock somewhere."

Tips 328-329
Go south of
disorder.

- **Tip 328 Set up a tailgate party.**
- **Tip 329 Sing karaoke.**

Tip 330
Cuddle on
a date.

— *Plan a romantic getaway*

I asked Rhonda (my wife) what would be romantic to do for Valentine's Day. I'm a man, so of course I need ideas for romance. She said a picnic would be romantic. I began to plan. I really thought a picnic on top of a skyscraper in downtown Dallas would be great, but I didn't have the connections to make it happen. (Do any of you have the right connections? If you do, let me know.)

The next best thing to having a picnic on a skyscraper was having a picnic on the fifth story of a parking garage in Sherman. The best seats in the house — atop my Ford 150 pickup — afforded a view of the city lights, and the gentle hum of the hospital generator provided "atmosphere."

As we cuddled with our blankets, pillows, wine, cheese, and Snickers, we were having fun!

— *Spice up a meal*

BUON GIORNO

(*Buon Giorno* means "Good morning" in Italian)

Isn't it fun to travel? Why does travel seem to balance out our stressful lives? When and where will you take your next trip?

In celebration of our 22-year anniversary, my wife and I recently made time for our dream trip to Italy. We traveled to Naples, Rome, and the Isle of Capri.

One highlight of our trip was the element of adventure. We traveled on planes, trains, buses, cable cars, boats, ferries, taxis, and subways. Here, we are used to jumping in our cars and driving to our destination. In Europe you must learn how to use public transportation. Yes, we got lost a lot, but every time we did, I would say to my wife, "It's another adventure!" To me it was energizing, refreshing, and fun!

A second highlight was the food. Naples is where pizza was created. There, pizzas come out of wood ovens and have perfectly crisp edges and tasty toppings of cheese, tomatoes, and basil. Another favorite is gelato, kind of like sweet and creamy homemade ice cream. We splurged and tasted all kinds of flavors. (It's good we burned calories by walking a lot.)

Don't wait — take time to travel. Balance the road of life by enjoying the journey now. Travel is a great adventure, full of tasty treats.

Arrivederci

**Tip 331
Make finger foods for dinner and feed each other.**

Tips 332-334
Explore new horizons.

• **Tip 332 Take that dream vacation.**

• **Tip 333 Ride on a cable car, a train, a gondola — something you've never tried before.**

• **Tip 334 Eat some pizza or ice cream with your significant other.**

My wife and I were watching a fun sitcom called *The King of Queens*. The couple was arguing, feeling distant, and wondering if they still had anything in common. Then they had an idea: Both would write a list of 20 things they liked to do and compare the lists.

Rhonda and I decided to make lists, too. At first we giggled because it was harder than we thought to think of 20 fun activities. Finally we completed our lists and shared them with each other. The sharing was half the fun. Wow, we had 11 fun activities (that's 55 percent) out of 20 in common. Those activities were: reading, travel, going out with friends, tasting new wines, hosting parties, going to church, watching a movie together, going out to a nice dinner, cooking/grilling together, swimming/laying out in the sun, and exercising. We had more in common than we had realized.

In *The King of Queens*, the couple only came up with one fun activity in common. Though disappointed, they made a commitment to be on the lookout for fun activities they could share.

Remember, playful balance is having fun activities that you can enjoy alone, with friends, and with your significant other.

Tip 335
Top twenty

— Take turns writing 20 fun activities and then share.

Have you ever noticed how marriage is hard, hectic, and many times hilarious?

- **Tip 336 Bring home fast food and serve it on your best china.**
- **Tip 337 Play frisbee together.**
- **Tip 338 Pack a picnic and then go star gazing.**
- **Tip 339 Dress up sexy and sip fancy cocktails at a hotel bar.**
- **Tip 340 Candles. Champagne. Bubble bath for two. Need I say more!**
- **Tip 341 Listen to live entertainment instead of a movie.**
- **Tip 342 Attend a one night class at the college together.**
- **Tip 343 Take a tour of garage sales in the ritziest neighborhoods.**
- **Tip 344 Have a kissing challenge—100 kisses in three hours.**
- **Tip 345 Go to or create your own drive-in movie.**

Tip 336-345 Take turns thinking of a fun date that costs very little money.

Coming up with a fun date can strain the brain. My buddy and I thought that taking our wives to a drive-in movie would score major brownie points with them. We bought the movie Grease with John Travolta and Olivia Newton-John. We iced down some Coca-Colas, popped some microwave popcorn, and set up a 13-inch TV/VCR in my grandmother's garage. We took our wives cruising around town before pulling up to the garage door. With the push of a few buttons, the garage door opened, the truck windows rolled down, and the movie came on. Both of our wives agreed we needed to read *Dating for Dummies*.

To make up for that impressive date, my wife asked me the next morning to make the bed. Do you realize how hard this task is for the average middle-aged man? It's like putting together a 5,000-piece jigsaw puzzle . . . while wearing boxing gloves. I barely know how to tuck in the sheets and pull the bedspread smooth, let alone arrange 237 pillows. Schwoo! Tell me, when did making a bed become so complicated?

Tips 346-347 Drive each other crazy.

• **Tip 346 Make the bed or put together a jigsaw puzzle.**

• **Tip 347 Dance in the closet with your honey.**

Marriage is hard and sometimes hectic. I found that out when I hurriedly ventured barefoot into our walk-in closet to retrieve a party dress. (Hey, the dress was for my wife.) Next to some dirty laundry, out of my sight, lurked a predator: a very high heel. Ouch! Woo! Ugh! I jumped up and down on my one good foot, trying to escape any more deadly creatures. Guess who walked in and found me dancing in the closet? My wife took one look and said, "Honey you're just falling in love, head over HEELS." (That was corny, I agree.)

Embarrassed and limping, I was ready to escape to the golf course. But of course I get a lot of grief for golf-related goofs, too.

For instance, after a round of golf my face is usually red with sunburn because I forget to lather on sunscreen. My wife will graciously point out that I'm getting wrinkles or crow's-feet around my eyes and, of course, looking much, much older than her. So how can I look younger? While watching Oprah, my wife discovered and bought me a fountain of youth miracle ointment. Was it Oil of Olay? Oh, no. Was it Estee Lauder? Absolutely not! It was a poor man's Botox, also known as Preparation H! In case you didn't know, this product is intended for a place … that is not … your face. Do you think there was a hidden message? After I used it for months my wife said, "Are you still using that stuff?" I can't believe you fell for that.

As Larry "the cable guy" says, "I don't care what you say, that there is FUNNY!"

The fact is I that did fall for that, just as many of us fall in love and fall for marriage. If your head is hurting about how hard and hectic marriage becomes, then remember to look high for the hilarious silver lining.

— Have fun

HOLIDAY PLAY

> **Tip 348**
> **Play a practical joke on your spouse. Be careful!**

Guess which holiday I have the most fun on? You got it — April Fools' Day!

April Fools' Day began in the 16th century when the beginning of the year was changed from April 1 to Jan. 1. Many people were clueless about the change and looked like fools. April 1 became the day to play tricks and pranks for fun.

Did you play any April Fools' jokes this year?

I was playfully privileged to be the "jester" for a Toastmaster contest on April 1. I demonstrated a little magic when I turned a yellow handkerchief into an egg. "That's not a real egg," someone said. I had him hold out his palms and dropped the egg yolk onto them. Of course, everyone whooped and hollered. At least no one got egg on their face.

A counselor whose work I supervise and I were meeting on April Fools' Day. I stopped the conversation and said, "Jeff, there's something serious we need to talk about. I was notified by my licensing board that I did not turn in the correct paperwork to be your supervisor. That means the last year that I have been supervising you is not going to count toward your supervision hours."

I was proud of Jeff as a counselor because he stayed calm and objective on the outside, though later he told me he was going bonkers on the inside. I then mischievously shouted, "April Fools!"

My last practical joke of the day came when a company representative e-mailed to ask me to facilitate a workshop for another well-known company. I have worked with this man for several years. I e-mailed him back the following:

> Marlin,
>
> I have sad bad news. My truck, which is my only form of transportation, was stolen. My wife's car was sucked up in a tornado last night. I'm going crazy!
>
> I'm sooooo depressed that I can't see myself ever leading another workshop in my miserable existence. Tell the company I'm sorry.
>
> P.S. Don't believe a word I said. APRIL FOOLS! Count me in for any company that needs a foolish facilitator!

Marlin e-mailed me back:

> Hi Brent,
>
> That was funny, and you had me totally "fished" in until you said you were going crazy.
>
> Thanks, I needed a good laugh today. I will definitely recommend YOU as a foolish facilitator always! Marlin

I realize that not everyone enjoys practical jokes. It is also true that we can go too far and we must keep the balance with our humor.

The other side of the coin is humor can help YOU keep the balance!

Tips 349-351 Play April Fools' jokes.

- **Tip 349 Learn a magic trick.**
- **Tip 350 Send a fun e-mail to someone today.**
- **Tip 351 Be a foolish facilitator in your next speaking opportunity..**

Is your funny bone itching for some Halloween humor? Enjoy these lighthearted stories compiled by Amy Zerello.

Trick or Tryst?

Desperate for a Halloween costume to wear to a party, my 43-year-old daughter had an inspired idea. She put on a slinky black dress and fishnet stockings and balanced a small tabletop on her head. On it was a lamp, a champagne glass, and an ashtray with two cigarette butts. She went as a one-night stand. And won first prize.

Contributed by **Sandra Campbell**

Private Party

It was Halloween night when a driver called our road-service dispatch office complaining that he was locked out of his car. I forwarded the information to a locksmith, along with one more detail: The car was parked at a nudist colony. Of course, the locksmith arrived in record time. But when he called in later, he wasn't amused. "Figures," he said. "I finally get to go to a nudist colony, and they're having a costume party!"

Contributed by **Neil Klein**

Mummified Mom

Last year my daughter and her children were invited to a Halloween party. Her older son wanted to go as Count Dracula; her daughter as a ballerina; her younger son as the cabin boy in Treasure Island. Then my daughter donned her own costume, wrapping herself in strips of white sheeting. At the party she collapsed, exhausted, on the sofa. "And who are you?" someone asked her. "I'm a tired mummy," my daughter replied.

Contributed by **Corinne Morse**

I've Created a Monster!

For Halloween, my grandson wanted to be The Incredible Hulk. Using food coloring and a washcloth, my daughter dyed his hands, face, neck, and blond hair the green shade of the TV monster.

After his bath the next morning, a faint green tint remained. As my grandson was going out the door to school, he handed his mother a slip of paper he had forgotten to give her earlier. My daughter quickly opened the note.

School pictures were going to be taken that day.

Contributed by **Ruth H. Smith**

Don't Play With Fire

As firefighters, we are required to wear our full bunker gear on all safety calls, even to advise homeowners of a county ordinance against burning leaves after dark. Last Halloween, two co-workers waited on the porch of one such offending household, helmets in hand, until a woman finally opened the door. Promptly dropping a candy bar into each helmet, she remarked, "You boys are a little old for this sort of thing, aren't you?" and closed the door.

Contributed by **Steve Farmer**

Climate Control

Everyone at the company I worked for dressed up for Halloween. One fellow's costume stumped us. He simply wore slacks and a white T-shirt with a large 98.6 printed across the front in glitter. When someone finally asked what he was supposed to be, he replied, "I'm a temp."

Contributed by **Brian Davis**

WORK PLAY

Recently I was the Toastmaster of the day (emcee for you non-Toastmasters). Attempting to make the meeting more fun, I created the theme "vacation on the beach."
I wore my surfer swimsuit, flip-flops, and a cabana hat. The Workforce boardroom (sometimes "bored" room) was transformed with palm trees, beach towels, and beach balls. To intensify our tan and protect us from the bright florescent lights, we lathered up with coconut oil and sunscreen. It was a vacation on the beach in the middle of the workday!

Why don't we foster a fun vacation atmosphere at work? Why not transform the serious to slightly silly?

I had a full schedule of clients (most of you know I'm a family therapist) to see that afternoon after the Toastmaster meeting. Bing. Bong. Believe it or not, I had an idea! Why not continue to wear my beach garb and decorate my counseling office with the "vacation on a beach" theme?

My clients needed a beach break from all the STRESS in their lives. They needed a casual, comfortable, "humor-contagious" climate to create courage to deal with their issues. As their therapist, I could model how to break out of the boredom box and balance with playfulness.

If your serious side is wondering how this could ever happen in a workplace, you're not alone. I had my doubts about my professionalism, but I discovered my clients were crazy about the "vacation on the beach" experience. My co-workers raved about the creative idea and want to plan a joint theme for a week in the office complex.

By now you're probably having ideas about how you could help your workplace "fun suckers" hop off the treadmill of seriousness and jump onto the trampoline of playfulness!

**Tips 352-354
Hop off the
treadmill of
seriousness.**

- **Tip 352 Have a vacation theme at your next work meeting.**

- **Tip 353 Decorate your work cubicle or office with fun items.**

- **Tip 354 Have a hat day at work to lighten up and have some fun.**

Here are a few fun quips excerpted from The Treasury of Business Humor written by James E. Myers.

"It's so difficult to soar like eagles when you work with turkeys."

"Be awful nice to 'em goin' up, because you're gonna meet 'em all comin' down." —Jimmy Durante

"To err is human. To really foul things up requires a computer!"

"Being at work on time, every day, is one way to assure your job and . . . that you'll be first to hear most of the gossip."

"My boss's secretary is a truly direct, honest person. The other day, a visitor came in to see the boss and his secretary said: 'Please tell me . . . would you care to be seated or should I book you into the nearest hotel?' "

"A good secretary can do a whole lot more than take dictation, type, and make coffee. She must also be able to create the illusion that the boss is in charge."

"My secretary sure did cure me of having her select gifts for my wife. How? Well, last December, she bought her a red BMW!"

**Tips 355-356
Write for fun.**

- **Tip 355 Write your own funny one-liners about your workplace.**

- **Tip 356 Have a contest and share your one-liners at a luncheon.**

E-mail is one major way most of us stay connected in the business world.

Recently, I was e-mailing a business associate about participating in an upcoming telephone conference. We decided on 9 a.m. Eastern time, which translated to 8 a.m. Central time for me. Reluctantly, I agreed on the early time on one condition—that my associate would provide me coffee. She sent me the following e-mail reply. *Thanks! Here is your coffee...*

After giggling, I e-mailed her back, saying, *I like cream with my coffee.* She sent me the following reply. *Here you go, you'll have to make your own.*

Now I was slapping my leg and laughing out loud! I sent her my final reply.

Mooooooo . . . You got me! Thanks for the laugh and playful break in the middle of the day.

Find creative ways to add fun, laughter, and playfulness in your e-mails. It will add balance to your day.

- **Tip 357 Add a humorous quote on your e-mail signature.**

- **Tip 358 Add playful pictures with your e-mails.**

**Tips 357-359
E-mail
for fun.**

- **Tip 359 Share a playful e-mail with someone you have talked to but never met.**

PLAY IN HARD TIMES

Charlie Chaplin once said, "Life is a tragedy when seen in close up, but a comedy in long shot."

It is frequently true what author Allen Klein said: "Sometimes we do not see the importance of laughter in our dark times because we are so blinded by our tears."

Aren't you amazed when people are able to use humor in times of trauma, tragedy, and death?

A speaker friend of mine recently shared her ordeal with breast cancer and mastectomy. She called her speech "DiscomBOOBulated." She joked about milking people's sympathy and using cancer as an excuse to not have to talk to people on the phone, especially the ones she didn't want to talk to. She also poked fun at how people hadn't paid this much attention to her chest since when she was breastfeeding her twins. Anne inspires me with her humorous twist on cancer and how "anyone who laughs lasts."

A recent counseling client shared with me how she was getting her will and her funeral and burial plans together. She raved about her "shopping" experience of buying a casket. She wanted to make sure she had a modest, but elegant casket for her going-away party. I asked her if she had purchased her burial clothes. "Heavens no," she said. "I don't want to be out of style." My client taught me that death does not have to be such a "grave affair."

ANYONE WHO LAUGHS, LASTS

I'll never forget when Vietnam veteran Dave Roever spoke at my church many years ago. Dave's face and body were disfigured when he was hit by a phosphorous grenade in the war. Dave shared his story of agony and how the experience had changed his entire life. He then sat down at the piano and stated that he could now miraculously play the piano by ear. He then surprised the congregation by literally removing his right ear and banging it on the piano keys. This is true self-effacing humor.

One of my clients recently lost her best friend to a tragic accident. She had the difficult job of going through her friend's belongings, clothes, and shoes and giving them away. The shoes did not fit any family member or friend, yet were the exact size for my grieving client. With tears in her eyes and a smile on her face, she said, "Dana always wanted me to feel like Cinderella." A Chinese proverb states, "You cannot prevent the birds of sorrow from flying over your head, but you can prevent them from building nests in your hair."

How do you keep your sense of humor, optimism, and playfulness in hard times?

My client had been bored to death in the county jail. In his spare time he caught a lizard that climbed through the bathroom drain. All of the cell mates quickly adopted this new jailhouse pet and named him Pimp Skinny.

The cellmates built a house for Pimp Skinny out of toilet paper. They were having fun taking care of Pimp Skinny, and I'm sure training him for future lucrative Broadway shows.

Then Pimp Skinny became lethargic and appeared sick. The inmates assumed that Pimp Skinny was getting too cold. My client attempted to warm Pimp Skinny by laying him on the stainless-steel toilet lid since hot water runs through the toilet. The unthinkable happened. Pimp Skinny died. The cellmates charged my client with first-degree murder.

But the angry cellmates found enough connection in their hearts to bake a birthday cake for my client. They bought cinnamon rolls from the commissary and flattened them on a piece of foil. After spreading a chocolate paste over the rolls, they topped the cake with Butterfinger crumbles and Snicker morsels. They "baked" the cake on the top of the stainless-steel toilet lid. My client said the cake was delicious.

Laughter removes chains and creates new freedom!
Anis Chin

My wife and I recently visited Aspen, Colorado on vacation and heard an interesting story of a burial. A famous author had died from cancer and had requested to be cremated and then shot out of a cannon from the top of the mountain. His ashes were scattered over the beautiful mountainside that he loved so much. When I heard the true story, I said, "Now that's going out with a bang! That author knew how to write a happy ending."

Remember the words of George Bernard Shaw: "Life does not cease to be funny when people die any more than it ceases to be serious when people laugh."

Tips 360-365 Keep laughing through the hard times.

- **Tip 360 Create your own "punny" words like "discomboobulated."**

- **Tip 361 Recall a funny story of how someone poked fun at their health problem.**

- **Tip 362 Share the story of Pimp Skinny with someone who needs a laugh.**

- **Tip 363 Share your funny thoughts about death.**

- **Tip 364 Put on a clown nose and act out Robin Williams from the movie Patch Adams**

- **Tip 365 Write a happy ending for your life that makes others laugh.**

ON BALANCE:

- Play heals you and others.
- Don't be so full of adult there is no child in you.
- Humor adds compound interest in the work place.
- Humor transforms our difficult times.

WHAT'S IN IT FOR ME?

_____

_____

_____

_____

_____

Authors Conclusion

Balance is woven in the fabric of creation. The rising and setting of the sun. The ebb and flow of the ocean waves. The changing seasons from winter, spring, summer, and fall. The earth spins around the galaxy and yet no one falls off the earth.

The reality is as humans we do tumble and fall off the tight rope of life. Achieving balance is not a destination rather an ongoing process. We gain balance by going to extremes and then centering to the middle. Life balance is about tumbling then becoming aware of our falling which brings us back to walking on the tight rope. When you fall and struggle in your journey of balance remember the following quote.

Be patient with everyone, but above all with yourself. I mean, do not be disheartened by your imperfections, but always rise up with fresh courage. How are we to be patient in dealing with our neighbor's faults if we are impatient in dealing with our own? He who is fretted by his own failings will not correct them. All profitable correction comes from a calm, peaceful mind.

St. Francis de Sales

Balance is not stillness. The faster you live, the greater your dreams, the more dynamic your vision, the greater our need for balance! Remember that life balance is always personal, always

professional, and forever playful! Balance will always give you coordination, courage, and confidence to ride the waves of life. I have enjoyed my ride with you. Please keep in touch and share your ups and downs at brent@brentspeaks.com. Truly we all know together Balance Matters !

Sometimes you reach a point of being so coordinated, so completely balanced, that you feel you can do anything— anything at all. At times like this I find I can run up to the front of the board and stand on the nose when pushing out through a broken wave; I can goof around, put myself in an impossible position and then pull out of it, simply because I feel happy. An extra bit of confidence like that can carry you through, and can do things that are just about impossible.

Midget Farrelly, champion surfer

How to contact Brent O'Bannon, MBS

Office 903-813-0723

Cell   903-819-0301

Fax   903-813-5452

Email:
brent@brentspeaks.com

Web: www.brentspeaks.com

Resources & Products Available:

• *The Balance Matters eZine* (free monthly email newsletter)

• Keynotes/training/workshops

• Personal Counseling

• Phone/email coaching

• Books, articles & audio programs

• (Go to www.brentspeaks.com to resources/products page for details)

Book Evaluation

Book Title: *Balance Matters: 365 Life Balance Tips!*
Fax to: 1-903-813-5452 Care of Brent O'Bannon

Please take a few minutes to fill out and fax this evaluation form. Your comments will be used to improve Balance Matters updates.

1. APPRAISAL OF BOOK CONTENT:	HIGH				LOW
a. To what degree did the content meet a need in which you expressed interest:	5	4	3	2	1
b. How much VALUE did you receive from this book?	5	4	3	2	1
c. Would you recommend this book to others who are interested in the subject area?	5	4	3	2	1
d. Based on the stated objectives, did this book meet your expectations?	5	4	3	2	1

2. AUTHOR EVALUATION:	EXCELLENT				POOR
a. Style and delivery	5	4	3	2	1
b. Application to real life	5	4	3	2	1
c. Knowledge of subject matter	5	4	3	2	1
d. Amount of humor	5	4	3	2	1

3. OVERALL EVALUATION: EXCELLENT   POOR

a. What is your overall evaluation of the book?   5   4   3   2   1

b. What were the MOST effective segments? Why?

_____

_____

_____

_____

c. What were the LEAST effective segments? Why?

_____

_____

_____

_____

d. Write a one to three sentence comment on what the seminar did for
you:

_____

_____

_____

_____

References

Berglas, Steven. *Reclaiming the Fire*, Random House, NY: 2001.

Blanchard, Ken, Thad Lacinak, Chuck Tompkins, and Jim Ballard. *Whale Done!*, Free Press, NY: 2002.

Cook, Marshall J. *Time Management*, Adams Media Corporation, MA: 1998.

Covey, Stephen. *The 7 Habits of Highly Effective People*, Fireside Simon & Schuster, NY: 1989.

Crawford, Roger. *How High Can You Bounce?*. Bantam Books, NY: 1998.

Glouberman, Dina. *The Joy of Burnout*, Inner Ocean, HI: 2002.

Gorkski, Terrance T. *Keeping the Balance*, Herald House/Independent Press, MO: 1993.

Hansen, Richard, Allyn Kramer, and Larry Upshaw. *Credibility Power*, Prestonwood Press, TX: 2001.

Hmachek, Don. *Encounters with the Self,* Harcourt Brace Jovanovich, FL: 1992.

Horn, Sam. *Tongue Fu!*. St. Martin's Griffin, NY: 1996.

Jones, Laurie Beth, *Jesus Life Coach*, Thomas Nelson Publishers, TN: 2004.

Leiter, Michael P. and Christina Maslach. *Banishing Burnout*, Jossey Bass, CA: 2005.

Leiter, Michael P. and Christina Maslach. *The Truth about Burnout*, Jossey Bass, CA: 1997.

Levey, Joel and Michelle Levey. *Living in Balance*, MJF Books, NY:1998.

Marriott, J.W. Jr. and Kathi Ann Brown. *The Spirit To Serve*, Harper Perennial, NY: 1997.

Maslach, Christina. *Burnout*, Malor, MA: 2003.

McGinnis, Alan Loy. *The Balanced Life*, Augsburg Fortress, MN: 1997.

Maxwell, John C. *Winning with People*, Nelson Publishers, TN: 2004.

Maxwell, John C. *The 17 Essential Qualities of a Team Player*, Nelson Publishers, TN: 2002.

Potter, Beverly. *Overcoming Burnout*, Ronin Publishing, CA: 2005.

Potter, Beverly. *Finding a path with a heart*, Ronin Publishing, CA: 1995.

Potter, Beverly. *Preventing Job Burnout*, Crisp Publications, CA: 1996.

Segel, Rick and Darren LaCroix. *Laugh & Get Rich*, Specific House Publishing, MA: 2000.

Skovholt, Thomas M. *The Resilient Practitioner*, Allyn and Bacon, MA: 2001.

Warren, Rick. *The Purpose Driven Life*, Zondervan, MI: 2002.

Weiten, Wayne and Margaret Lloyd. *Psychology Applied to Modern Life*, Brooks/Cole Publishing, CA: 1997.

Book Order Form

Email orders: brent@brentspeaks.com

Fax orders: (903) 813-5452- Send this form.

Telephone orders: (903) 813-5452- Have your credit card ready.

Postal orders: Brent O'Bannon 115 S. Travis, Suite 303 Sherman, TX 75090

Please send me _____ copies of *Balance Matters* at $19.97 each, plus shipping and handling.

Please send me FREE information on:

❏ Speaking/seminars ❏ Coaching/Counseling

❏ Audio Programs ❏ Balance Matters eZine

Name: _____

Address: _____

City: _____ State: _____

Zip: _____ Phone: _____

Email: _____

Sales tax: Please add 8% for products shipped to Texas addresses.

Shipping: US: $4 for the first book or audio program and $2 for each additional product. International: $9 for 1st book or audio program; $5 for each additional product.

Payment: Check enclosed ❏

Credit card : Visa ❏ MasterCard ❏ American Express ❏

Card number: _____

Name on card: _____

Signature: _____

Exp. Date: _____/_____

Publishing

Audio Resource Order Form

You may fax your order to: (903) 813-5452

Please check the items you wish to order:

Title	Price
❏ Winning in Everyday Life audio CD	$20.00

❏ Balance Pack $40.00
Includes: *The 7 Habits of a Balance Master*
2 CD set and Downloadable Workbook
The 7 Habits of a Balance Master

❏ Care Pack $40.00
Includes: *Dealing with Difficult People*
The Art of CAREfrontation
Downloadable handouts

❏ Power Pack $100.00
Includes: *Winning in Everyday Life* audio CD
The 7 Habits of a Balance Master
2 audio set· *Dealing with Difficult People*
The Art of CAREfrontation

Your Total $_____

Name: _____

Address: _____

City: _____ State: _____

Zip: _____ Phone: _____

Email: _____

Credit card : Visa ❏   MasterCard ❏   American Express ❏

Card number: _____

Name on card: _____

Signature: _____

Exp. Date: _____/_____

THANK YOU FOR YOUR PURCHASE!!!